THE
ABCs
OF BEING MOM

THE
ABCs
OF BEING MOM

**ADVICE AND SUPPORT FROM
THE MOM NEXT DOOR**

Birth through Kindergarten

KAREN BONGIORNO

SHE WRITES PRESS

Published 2021
Printed in the United States of America
Print ISBN: 978-1-64742-010-9
E-ISBN: 978-1-64742-011-6
Library of Congress Control Number: 2020921887

For information, address:
She Writes Press
1569 Solano Ave #546
Berkeley, CA 94707

Interior design by Tabitha Lahr

She Writes Press is a division of SparkPoint Studio, LLC.

For my dear husband and children
and for loving moms everywhere.

CONTENTS

INTRODUCTION

I t started in the delivery room, when I became a mother on a gorgeous October day that sparkled with autumn's vibrancy. Such a day had to be filled with possibility and promise! And it was, because at 5:57 p.m. on that October day, my first child, my daughter, entered the world two weeks before her November due date.

She arrived crying, no doubt letting us know that she was not happy to have been squeezed out and cut loose from her warm, secure haven of the last eight and a half months, and deposited without a warning into this bright, cold, wide-open space. The doctor and nurses ignored her cries and began attending to her newborn requirements: the routine Apgar tests for vital signs and responsiveness, recordings of her weight and length, and imprints of her tiny, perfect feet.

That's when it happened: I began to worry. I didn't see the instruction manual! Wasn't it supposed to be attached to her ankle in a waterproof bag? Without that guide, how would I ever become a good mom who was capable of raising a balanced and happy child?

While I was pregnant, I'd read numerous books explaining my baby's daily natal development. I'd eaten the necessary foods to provide the right vitamins, proteins, and minerals for my growing baby. I'd baked my own healthy snacks, taken the prescribed neonatal vitamins, and given up caffeine and alcohol. I'd gone to my OB/GYN appointments with a list of questions to make certain my baby-to-be was growing properly. Both my husband and I took Lamaze classes and even a baby CPR class. I'd followed all the doctors' and experts' advice in the books I read, to ensure that my baby would enter the world healthy. But *now* I needed the sequel to tell me what I needed to know about motherhood itself.

I worried as the nurses were busy cleaning my daughter. They secured her in the standard newborn hospital blanket—white with faded stripes of narrow pink and thick blue. Next, they topped her head with a tiny knit hat. By now she was warm and swaddled and had stopped crying, but I could not stop shaking. My adrenal hormones were causing my body to react after labor, although I didn't know this at the time. I wondered what was happening. I asked the doctor and labor nurses, "When does the shaking stop?"

A male nurse answered cheerfully, "Not until they go off to college," as if to say, *Lots of luck, lady, we just deliver the babies. Now off you go and just get on with it.*

I wrote the *THE ABCs OF BEING MOM* to help you as you "get on with" your journey of loving, nurturing, teaching, guiding, and raising your child from the day she or he is born until the day he or she leaves for college. Because, with the arrival of your baby, whether you are your child's birth mother or adoptive mother, your life as you knew it has changed. Completely.

There are many books that tell all about babies and what to expect when you are pregnant. Many books explain the developmental stages your baby, toddler, child, and adolescent will go through, and how he or she will transform physically and emotionally in each stage. *THE ABCs OF BEING MOM*, however, is not one of those. *THE ABCs OF BEING MOM* was written specifically for moms, telling you what it's like to be Mom, taking you through the various stages of motherhood, telling you what to watch out for and what's likely to come next.

Moms encounter a full spectrum of emotions. We worry, question, doubt, cheer, become confused, agonize, praise, and feel proud, happy, blessed, delighted, angry, and sad—sometimes all in the same day. We learn and assimilate as we grow and pass through phases. For the most part, we begin our journey with no experience, adapting and learning as we go. We take on roles and responsibilities as they present themselves.

Before becoming a mother, we heard people say, "Motherhood is wonderful!" This is true, but we could not fully understand this because we had not yet experienced motherhood. Motherhood is a different kind of wonderful; it completely engulfs us, filling our hearts and souls with devoted passion and love for our children. It plants us deeply in a field, where we grow and feel the warmth, connection, and joy of loving freely and absolutely.

As mothers, we learn we need support on our journey of raising our children. We discover that caring for our children brings new challenges, questions, and added layers of detail and information to keep track of. Our priorities change, as do our views and outlook. Our world, hearts, and knowledge expand. We master one phase or role and are regularly faced with new ones to figure out and take on.

We don't get much feedback on our efforts or know if what we are experiencing is normal. We have no frame of reference. At times we feel confident and happy in being Mom. Other times we falter and have fears about how to handle the circumstances and situations we face. Sometimes we just feel exhausted or overwhelmed by the chaos and disarray in our lives and homes. If we *do* have time to pause for reflection, we recognize how much meaning came into our lives when we became Mom and how special it is to be Mom. Above all, we know we love our children and want them to be happy.

This is certainly how being a mother has been for me. While raising my children, I loved them fiercely, but I did a lot of worrying—something I'd not done much of before. By nature, I am an optimist and a hard worker, and I'd made my way through adult life this way—working hard at each stage, expecting I'd do fine and would continue this way. I'd taken each step, from being a college student and then a graduate, to beginning a successful career, to building a happy marriage. This had added up to a reasonably balanced life. But all this changed when I became a mother. I was still an optimist, but I was no longer balanced, and I'd become a worrier.

The epiphany that your life really *has* changed doesn't occur until your baby arrives. When you were pregnant or preparing to adopt your child, people probably told you, "Motherhood is life changing." At that time, your thoughts might have been something like, *Well, obviously! I'll have my own adorable baby. We'll have fun hanging out while she or he grows naturally into being a wonderful and accomplished adult.* But then your baby arrives and it hits you—*Now what?*

In the pages of *THE ABCs OF BEING MOM,* I go with you on your journey of raising your child, giving you the knowledge and the perspective I've gained in the last twenty-plus years of raising my daughter and son. Both went on to college and are thriving—despite my husband and I raising them while climbing steep learning curves, gaining knowledge haphazardly, and muddling through mistakes due to inexperience.

THE ABCs OF BEING MOM is a three book series that covers the years your child will live with you, from birth to young adult. My purpose in writing these books was to give you the guide I was looking for in the delivery room when my daughter was born. This book, Book One, begins with the adjustments and tentativeness you feel as a new mother. It guides you through those beginning years, the toddler years, the preschool years, and ends with your child's kindergarten year. Book Two travels with you on the long road of your child's grade school years, through elementary and middle school. Book Three accompanies you during the very full high school years when your child is changing rapidly, and there is so much compressed into those four years. It includes college prep guides for your child and concludes with reflections on the journey you've taken as Mom.

You'll see that I celebrate the pleasures and acknowledge the difficulties of motherhood throughout these books. At each stage, I provide insights and helpful observations. I emphasize the importance of support within your family and the surrounding community. Use this knowledge to form your own perspective.

My wish is that my books will give you answers and ease the worries that come with the emotions and challenges of being Mom. I hope they give you comfort and confidence in yourself—allowing you, despite "the shaking," to embrace motherhood as wonderful—with the knowledge that your dear child will treasure and love you as her own unique and special mother, on this, your incredible, life-changing journey.

USING THIS BOOK

You'll see that I alternate referring to your child as he in one chapter and as she in the following chapter. This tactic avoids the need to refer to your child using the awkward phrase he/she. In *Chapters One* and *Two,* I also refer to your child as Baby or your baby. At the end of each chapter, you'll find a summary of suggestions, tips, and reference information for the age and stage described in that particular chapter.

Book One includes an extensive chapter on family organization. In it, you'll find systems for organizing and managing day-to-day family living as well as tips to make everyday family life smoother. A calendar designed specifically to manage family life week by week anchors these systems with detailed instructions on using the calendar to keep control of your family's plans and needs. I've included tables of reference information by category that families need to have available, along with methods for storing and retrieving the information. And you'll find a chapter on family finances, budgeting, and safeguards to provide for your child.

At the end of the book, you'll find a list of resources for websites, articles, and books that may be helpful to you along the way. You can also find links to resources on my website, karenbongiorno.com.

My advice is to begin reading the chapter in this book that describes the age your child is now. I also recommend looking at the guidelines, suggestions, and resources mentioned in previous chapters. It's helpful to read each chapter slightly before your child reaches the next chapter's age. This will give you a sense of what's coming.

I hope you find encouragement in these books and happiness on your journey. My very best wishes and love to you, dear Mother, and your family.

In Chapter One:

THE FIRST THREE MONTHS

(your baby will be referred to as "he")

- O Congratulations on your new baby
- O New baby/new mother adjustments
- O Learning on the "job"
- O Value of pediatrician
- O Importance of caring for self
- O Watch for "baby blues"/postpartum depression
- O Diaper bag essentials
- O Delight in and enjoy your baby
- O TIPS AND SUGGESTIONS TABLE
- O REFERENCE INFORMATION TABLE

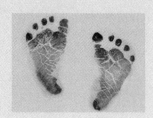

Chapter One

THE FIRST THREE MONTHS—
BEGINNING DAYS OF
MOTHERHOOD

YOUR BABY IS BORN!!

From here on, you will always be Mommy, Mom, Ma, Mamma, Mumsy, Mum, Momma, or another derivation of Mother. Congratulations! You did it! Your new life of being a mother has just begun, as has your new baby's. You are beginning your new lives together. This is a whole new experience filled with new demands. You will be learning on the job as you react to each new situation and circumstance. You will need to respond to unpredictable events with which you have no prior experience.

To begin with, you will be completely overpowered by the emotions you feel for this tiny, crying, vulnerable, beautiful new baby who has entered your life. You may feel nervous as you start down this unknown path of caring for your baby. He is no longer contained in his compact, self-nourishing, and self-sustaining environment. He has arrived accompanied by new products and gear, and with demands that need to be met around the clock. Simultaneously, he has taken over your heart and your life; his presence dominates your home.

Do not worry if you are overwhelmed. This is the normal way we begin motherhood, meeting it head-on. There is no slow start where we begin to warm our engines, taxi down the runway, gain speed gradually, and then take off, knowing we have reached sufficient speed to do so safely. Instead, we race at full speed down a short runway, burst into the sky, and avoid looking down. Keep flying. Nor is it like entering a river gradually, splashing at the edge, and wading in slowly before immersing ourselves for a pleasant swim. Rather, we must dive in, thrash about, tread furiously in order to keep our tiny new baby afloat and thriving. We do this while barely keeping our own head above water. Just keep swimming.

As a new mother, you will be subjected to continual and erratic awakenings. Inevitably you will become severely sleep-deprived, as your baby will make his needs known mostly by crying . . . often. Though fragile, your precious baby is nonetheless strong enough to insist that you satisfy his needs. Each time he cries, you will be motivated to respond, regardless of your exhausted or foggy physical and mental state. Your intense desire to stop his crying will compel you to respond to him immediately.

This is Mother Nature at work. She is responsible for the hormones within us that result in these intense and powerful emotions binding us to our babies and ensuring that our babies' care, comfort, needs, and demands will be satisfied.

Here is the origin of the fierce and primal bond that exists between us as mothers and children. This bond begins to develop during pregnancy, continues through labor and delivery, and culminates when we hold our baby in our arms. The first time each of us holds our baby as a mother, including adoptive mothers, we know with certainty the bond we have with our beautiful, tiny newborn is absolute, enduring, and cannot be severed by anyone or anything.* We feel this forcefully like a mother bear. Woe to anyone who might come between us and our cubs!

*Louann Brizendine, MD, discusses research on the transformations that occur in the brains of mothers, including adoptive mothers, to ensure the connection between mothers and their babies in her book *The Female Brain.*

During these beginning days of motherhood, all the nerves in your body will seem to be standing on end as you expend all your time and energy, mentally and physically caring for your infant. Your emotions will spiral between joy, exhaustion, and inadequacy. This is completely normal. You have just begun your life in this new world of *being Mom.*

Especially in your first days, it is important to do only the basics. This means sleep, eat, and repeat, for both you and Baby. Whether you are nursing or bottle-feeding your baby, he should be gaining weight and looking healthy. You will want to keep all your baby's appointments with his pediatrician and your appointments with your obstetrician, as they are extremely important to the health of your baby and of you.

Most likely, you will have chosen a pediatrician a couple of months or so before your baby was due. You will have

obtained referral(s) from your obstetrician or other trusted source, then
interviewed the pediatrician(s) to be
satisfied with your choice. Your pediatrician will visit and examine Baby
at the hospital. If you do not have a
pediatrician, get a recommendation
for one before you leave the hospital,
and be sure to schedule Baby's first
appointment.

> Your pediatrician
> should be someone
> you trust and feel
> comfortable with.
> He/she will likely
> be your partner
> in caring for your
> child's health and
> well-being for the
> next eighteen years.

Some doctors like to schedule an appointment within four
or five days of birth, others at two weeks. In the meantime,
if you have questions or worries, do not hesitate to call your
pediatrician. Do not worry about bothering him or her, or
about feeling silly or embarrassed by questions. You have no
experience in this new world of mothering; you only have
your instincts to rely on. Having your questions answered by
an experienced professional will give you comfort.

Your baby's health and your confidence in being a mother
will benefit by gaining knowledge and establishing a good
working relationship with your pediatrician. Conversations
and visits with the doctor in the first few weeks of your baby's
life are important for tracking his
growth and progress. These initial
appointments are vital to your
baby's health.*

> *Always schedule your
> next appointment
> before you leave the
> pediatrician's office.

Your pediatrician has the
experience to recognize seemingly insignificant signs that
indicate your baby requires attention. Recognizing and treating symptoms early will help avoid more severe complications.

This happened in my daughter's case. We were at an appointment when she was less than a week old. The pediatrician noticed that her skin looked slightly yellow, meaning she had a touch of jaundice. "Sunshine will rid her of the jaundice," he told me. "Place her infant seat by a window in your apartment where the sun will shine on her. Do this for a few days, and this will be enough to offset the jaundice." (And it did disappear within a couple of days. If her jaundice had been more severe, she would have needed additional care.)

Amid all the new excitement, demands, and upheaval that arrived with your new baby, you will need to remember to care for yourself. You are recovering from giving birth, and your body needs time to heal. If you had a difficult pregnancy or delivery, this recovery time will be all the more important. Follow your obstetrician's advice. Get rest whenever possible.

Ideally, you will have extra help from family, friends, or even health-care assistants. Visitors who come to help should do just that and not expect you to act as host. Others who come to congratulate you and see your new baby should realize you will not be able to spend much time socializing. Feel free to excuse yourself to rest or to be with Baby on your own. Your first priority is to yourself and Baby.

The joy of discovering you were pregnant and the care you took to be sure you gave birth to a healthy baby have been your primary focus and concern for the last nine months. Then came the happiness of bringing your baby home, receiving congratulatory gifts and flowers, and having visitors; all made you feel cherished and special. You reveled in the cuteness of the adorable baby clothes you received.

When the initial flurry of excitement ends, however, you and Baby will be on your own. Your spouse or partner will go back to work every day and may even be away, traveling for business. If you are a single mom, your visitors and helpers may now be gone. You may feel at loose ends, out of sync, and unsure of what comes next. You will not yet have a sense of routine in your new life.

At this point, it will be important for you to be kind to yourself regarding expectations. Do not expect to be "productive" or to immediately fit back into the life you had before your baby arrived. You will not be able to get things done or accomplish everything in the manner to which you were accustomed.

Your routines will be quite different, and customary habits will disappear. For example, just to take a shower, you will need to think ahead. Between feeding and changing Baby and other tasks you need to get done, you'll need to wait until a time when your baby is sleeping or happy in his infant seat. Then you can finally take a few minutes for yourself. You may not have time until four in the afternoon to take a hasty and unsatisfying shower. When you emerge, you might hear Baby crying for you. Scenarios such as this will occur and shouldn't make you feel as though you have failed as a mother.

You will not be able to anticipate every need your newborn has or be able to time his care perfectly. Babies fuss, cry, wail, and bawl; it's inevitable and unavoidable. Your baby is growing rapidly, which affects his sleep and appetite, changing his schedule and patterns. Don't feel you are a neglectful mother if Baby cries before you can attend to him. He is simply reminding you that he needs you—often crying frantically, as though he has been seriously neglected or abandoned.

You may not have any routines other than feeding, changing, and bathing Baby. But you will need to be conscientious about eating healthy and nutritious foods for your own good. This is extremely important if you are breastfeeding. Equally important is getting rest; this can be your biggest challenge. In the first few months, before your infant eats enough to go longer between feedings, you will be awakened every night at varying times to change and feed him. You will have to make up for sleep loss by taking naps whenever possible during the day. Caring for a newborn requires endurance and stamina.

> Your well-being is important. Care for yourself by eating well and getting sleep. Let go of doing nonessential things until you can get adequate rest and sleep.

When you are nursing or bottle-feeding your baby, pay attention to him. This is a critical time for bonding, understanding your baby, and learning how best to respond to him. Electronics are *very* addictive. So avoid using your phone for texting or catching up on e-mails or social media. You don't want them to interfere with your relationship with Baby.

> Bonding with Baby is central to his cognitive, social, and emotional development.

It's important to know that up to 80 percent of mothers will experience baby blues, according to the website webmd.com. If you find that you don't feel connected to your baby at first, you may be experiencing baby blues. Baby blues is a condition that can occur in the first few days of motherhood. Webmd.com notes that baby blues will contribute to many mothers feeling excessively emotional: suddenly happy, irritable, or sad. However, if these

POSTPARTUM DEPRESSION

1. POSTPARTUM DEPRESSION GUIDE

https://www.webmd.com/depression/postpartum-
depression/understanding-postpartum-depression-
basics#1

2. BABY BLUES OR POSTPARTUM DEPRESSION?

https://www.babycenter.com/0_the-baby-blues_11704.
bc#articlesection4

symptoms last past the first two weeks after bringing your baby home, you should discuss them with your doctor. Inexplicable sadness, irritability, or other extreme emotions that continue without any relief mean you need help. You may be suffering from postpartum depression (PPD), a condition that has severe consequences for your health, as well as your baby's health.

Postpartum depression could lead to neglect of your baby or harm to your baby or yourself. *See Box: Postpartum Depression.* You'll find a guide to understanding postpartum depression in the first website, webmd.com, and a short quiz that you can take to find out if you have signs of postpartum depression in the second website, babycenter.com. It's natural to feel frustrated or overwhelmed at times. If you ever feel desperate enough to consider being rough with your baby, you must get immediate attention to help you through this. There is no downside to asking for help. You may need help temporarily or perhaps longer, depending on your situation

DIAPER BAG ESSENTIALS

- ○ changing pad
- ○ extra diaper(s)
- ○ wipes
- ○ bottle (if bottle-feeding)
- ○ cloth diaper to cover Baby
- ○ toy/book for Baby to look at

- ○ Baby's special blankie
- ○ floor mat/blanket
- ○ extra house/apartment key
- ○ snack for Baby (when he begins to snack) and for you also

and your baby's temperament and condition. Doctors can prescribe medication to treat postpartum depression, even if you are breastfeeding. The important thing is to get support from family or friends *and* treatment from professionals right away.

Beyond feeding and providing clean diapers for Baby, a basic element of taking care of him will be getting him dressed and prepared to go out with you. Add getting someplace on time with Baby, and you will see that practice and experience are needed to manage this accomplishment competently. Getting to your baby's first appointment at the pediatrician's office on time will be a major outing and an opportunity to begin practicing this skill.

Before going out the door, you will need to have fed your baby, ensured his diaper is clean, gotten yourself dressed, and made sure you picked up the diaper bag to bring with you. If you thought about it, you will have stocked it with the essential items your baby might need while you are out. *See Box: Diaper Bag Essentials.* (A good time to restock it is before you go to bed each night. Put it at the door where you can grab it easily on your way out each day. This is helpful and can save

PEDIATRICIAN VISITS

○ Bring your list of questions
○ Be ready to share observations about your baby, how you are handling him, how you are doing
○ Take notes during your visit:
  - weight (percentile)
  - height/length (percentile)
  - immunizations
  - advice
  - follow-up care, if necessary
○ Schedule your baby's next appointment before you leave

you from last-minute scrambling to find an item, especially when you are running late or have become frazzled from an unexpected delay. Somehow, this happens quite often.)

You will have the list of questions you have prepared for the pediatrician. *See Box: Pediatrician Visits.* You will have dressed and bundled your baby appropriately for the weather. Next, you will head out to put him into his car seat. If things are going smoothly, and your baby is calm, you will not have banged your own or your baby's head while getting him into the car. You'll have been able to buckle him safely into his seat without him crying at the indignity of being placed and restrained where he can't reach you.

At last, you can get in the car to drive. Once you reach your destination, you'll get him out and put him in the new stroller, to which you, not to mention Baby, are still getting accustomed. You'll attach the diaper bag to the stroller some-how or maybe just sling it over your shoulder along with your regular handbag and then continue awkwardly into the pedi-atrician's office. At this point, you will be feeling a mixture of incompetence and satisfaction at having arrived safely and reasonably on time for your appointment. Score points for yourself. You and Baby made it!

As you begin to get a little more rest and sleep, make getting out and going somewhere each day a priority. This will give structure to your daily schedule. You might plan a walk to the store or a local coffee spot. You might decide to go for a drive or head to the park or shops. Going to the grocery or drugstore can be your outing for the day. This was my go-to location at least three or four times a week. Babies always need something: diapers, wipes, shampoo. Walking or driving to and from a destination provides a welcome change of pace, getting you out of your house or apartment and giving you and your baby the opportunity to see and interact with other people. This is good for both of you.

Your newborn will grow rapidly. Notice how his infant ways captivate you. Smile at the funny, snuffly sounds he makes when he is absorbed in eating. Breathe in his sweet baby smell when his head is resting on your shoulder after you have fed and burped him. Linger with your head against his, allowing these moments to seep deeply into your heart and be preserved as precious memories. Enjoy his irresistible cuddliness when he scrunches his body up and works to nestle further into your neck. See how you quickly reassure him when he startles abruptly.

> Delight in your baby. Enjoy these early days when you can.

You and Baby are learning about one another in elemental ways. You begin with seeing one another. You take in one another's face, shape, and presence. You grow used to feeling Baby in your arms, and he grows used to being lifted, held, cleaned, changed, dressed, and fed. You are amazed at the velvet softness of his skin. You want to cover his little face with kisses, kiss his hands, and gnaw gently on his tiny wrists. Baby recognizes your smell and your voice and feels secure. You begin to discern meanings for the different noises and cries he makes.

When you have a quiet moment, perhaps when your baby is settled in his crib and asleep, you may pause to look at Baby and reflect. Your baby is your miracle, a gift brought into the world with love. When he sleeps, he looks peaceful and content. You are filled with happiness and wonder that here he is—a brand-new person—with his whole life ahead of him. You know you will do your best to nurture, protect, and guide him, because you love him wholeheartedly.

When you are at home by yourself with your baby, you may begin to think, *I'd like to know other new mothers and newborns with whom I can share time.* But you may not know other new mothers in the area. This was the case for me. If you took a Lamaze or other kind of birthing class, contact one or two mothers from your class. See if one would like to meet, so you can take your infants for a walk or go for coffee (decaf, of course, if you are breastfeeding). You could ask your pediatrician's office and your hospital for information on "mommy and me" activities for infants. Just a few low-key outings are probably all you'll want to do or be able to manage, for now. I found a very small group of new mothers through my pediatrician. We met with our infants for about an hour each week to share our experiences and thoughts. As first-time mothers, this was about as much time as we had.

As I mentioned, your routine will consist mostly of changing and feeding your baby throughout the day and night. Even if you have help, it will be you, dear Mother, who has the primary responsibility for your baby's nourishment and care.

During these first months of motherhood, you'll have nights when you and your baby are the only ones awake. As tired as you feel, these middle-of-the-night periods are a quiet and contemplative time to connect with your baby. In my daughter's very early days, we were up late each night or in the very early morning hours when I fed her. One night, when my mind was hazy between wakefulness and sleep, I noticed how still it was outside our one-bedroom apartment on the seventeenth floor. The world seemed detached, as though my daughter and I were the only ones aware of time and our presence. I remember at that moment understanding the connection between my daughter and me—our innate bond. I felt certain I could do this—I could be Mom! As mothers, we feel this attachment inherently and understand this ancient and primal connection that encourages us to care for our beloved child.

You may have nights when you feel as though your baby is "wired" and will never get to sleep. You'll wonder how you became a participant in this senseless experiment to discover the minimal amount of sleep one needs to function. Your head will bob and jerk when you doze off for a moment; you'll realize you are still up, sitting on the couch or chair with your baby, who has no intention of falling asleep. You'll think longingly of lying in your bed. How much longer will it be before you can crawl gratefully under the covers? Tomorrow you will need extra rest. Your to-do items can always be rescheduled.

Nightly awakenings will not continue forever. Many babies will be able to sleep through the night by three months of age, and most will by nine months, according to the National Sleep Foundation. My daughter began sleeping through the night at exactly three months. My son was three years old before he slept through the night. Before then, he would sleep for a maximum of three or four hours at a time. Those years were an ongoing challenge, to say the least. Luckily, that kind of sleep pattern is not the norm for most babies.

Many mothers will go back to work, either full-time or part-time, after being home with their newborn for a few weeks or months. Whether your baby is at day care or being taken care of by your spouse or partner, a nanny, friends, or relatives, be sure the person who cares for Baby is competent, affectionate, gives you daily updates on your baby's day and activities, and lets you know about any emerging skills your child is trying to master. Down the road, as his world expands, you'll want to know how he is interacting with other children and caretakers, and what activities, toys, games, or books are fascinating to him.

Enjoy these first few months with Baby, despite new demands, learning curves, and sleep deprivation. Be proud of how you've learned to care for your newborn. It's become second nature for you to support your baby's head when you pick him up; to bathe him carefully, as you've learned that wet babies are very slippery; to cover your baby's sharp nails so he doesn't scratch himself. You know it's easier to clip your baby's nails when he is sleeping, and if you have a boy, to cover his privates when changing him, to avoid being sprayed.

The baby tornado that touched down in your home showered baby products, furnishings, and paraphernalia everywhere. Little clothes, diapers, hooded towels, burping cloths, baby blankets, swaddling blankets, baby toys, stuffed animals, soft books, and bottles, added to by baby shampoo, extra-gentle laundry soap, a Baby Bjorn, gifts from family and friends, baby monitors, as well as a changing table, crib, and stroller display overwhelming evidence of your baby's impact upon arrival. The unmistakable presence of your new family member is everywhere in your home. Hang on, Mom, and embrace this whirlwind journey. This is motherhood!

I've written suggestions that may be helpful for you during your baby's current stage. These suggestions are also shown in the tables *TIPS AND SUGGESTIONS—BY AGE AND STAGE* and *REFERENCE INFORMATION* at the end of the chapter. You'll see that the tips and suggestions are divided by category, for example, Your Baby's Well-Being, Your Well-Being, etc.

⬦⬦⬦⬦⬦⬦⬦⬦⬦⬦⬦⬦⬦⬦⬦⬦⬦⬦⬦⬦⬦⬦⬦⬦⬦⬦

Note: Beginning in *Chapter Two*, I will include tips, suggestions, and reference information in just the table format. Suggestions and information that are still useful will be carried forward into subsequent chapter tables.

Tips and Suggestions

○ Make it a rule to put your phone and other electronics aside when feeding your baby and during one-on-one time together. (As you know, they are addictive. You don't want them to interfere with the relationship you are developing with your baby.)

○ Don't try to get back into your pre-pregnancy-size clothes yet. They won't be comfortable. Wearing and even purchasing a few new maternity clothes makes more sense. If you buy larger "regular" clothes, they will be a waste of money. The proportions won't fit your immediate post-pregnancy body, and they will be too large once you go back to your pre-pregnancy weight. While breastfeeding, don't worry about weight loss; you will naturally shed extra pounds while breastfeeding. It took nine months to put on those pounds that brought your healthy baby. Be patient, and your "baby weight" will disappear.

○ Find pretty pajamas (constructed for nursing, if you are breastfeeding) to wear. You will spend many waking hours in them during nighttime feedings. You'll feel a little more "human" by wearing something attractive, despite the inhumane hours you are keeping. (Hold on to these pajamas; they will remind you of this time and the sweetness of new beginnings.)

Reference Information

After my baby was born, I realized I needed to collect and save some information to have for future reference. The information I suggest you save now is listed below. (Don't worry about how you save information. You can put it in a loose-leaf file, a notebook, or in notes/documents on your computer or smartphone.)

☆ YOUR BABY'S HEALTH RECORDS

Create a file for your baby's health records. Keep vaccination records and notes from the doctor and other health-care visits.

Vaccination Records: For a printable immunization schedule, go to: www.cdc.gov/vaccines/parents/downloads/milestones-tracker.pdf. Keep these updated; you will need them for reference. Your child will need these records even into adulthood. And it's surprising how many times you'll need this information for school, camp, and activity forms.

Notes from Doctors and Other Health-Care Visits: Date and take brief notes for each doctor visit you make with your baby. Writing things down is a good habit. Much of caring for your baby is new for you. Having notes you can refer to will be a relief when your mind is feeling cloudy, so you don't need to check back with the doctor or pediatric nurse when you are trying to remember, for example, what did the doctor say about your baby having "x" symptom? Should you check back if your baby has "x" symptom? Or does "x" symptom mean your baby is getting better? It is easy to forget details when you are overwhelmed with new feelings, experiences, and lack of sleep.

☆ REFERENCE PAGE FOR IMPORTANT CONTACTS

Create a reference page of contact information showing doctors, caregivers, emergency phone numbers, relatives, and neighbors. Post this in your home for babysitters and other caregivers.

TIPS AND SUGGESTIONS—THE FIRST THREE MONTHS	
YOUR BABY'S WELL-BEING	+ Put aside your phone and electronics when nursing or feeding your baby and during one-on-one time. + Talk to your baby.
YOUR WELL-BEING	+ Buy cozy, attractive pajamas so you can feel "halfway attractive," while the other half of you feels like a zombie during the long nights of caring for your newborn. + Don't try to get back into your pre-pregnancy clothes yet. + Buy clothes for nursing (if you are breast-feeding). + Be patient with yourself. It is enough for you to feed and take care of your baby and yourself each day.
YOUR VILLAGE/ COMMUNITY	+ Meet your neighbors if possible.

REFERENCE INFORMATION—THE FIRST THREE MONTHS
☆ SAVE LONG-TERM

☆ **BABY'S IMMUNIZATION RECORDS**
Keep track of your baby's immunizations.
Go to: www.cdc.gov/vaccines/parents/downloads/mile stones-tracker.pdf for a printable immunization schedule.

☆ **BABY'S HEALTH RECORDS—NOTES**
Keep the notes you take at pediatrician and other health-care appointments.

☆ **IMPORTANT CONTACTS REFERENCE LIST**
Create a contact list to post in your home for babysitters and other caregivers: include doctors, caregivers, hospital, emergency phone numbers, relatives, neighbors.

☆ **COMMUNITY GROUP(S)' MEMBERSHIP DIRECTORY(S)**
(if any)

In Chapter Two:

FOUR MONTHS TO ONE YEAR

(your baby will be referred to as "she")

○ New priorities

○ Employment flexibility considerations

○ No consensus on the benefits to children of employed mothers vs. stay-at-home mothers

○ New roles and routines—on-the-job training

○ Babies crave sociability

○ Getting out with Baby

○ Connect with other moms

○ Sharing tasks and responsibilities with your spouse/partner

○ Restorative time

○ Finding babysitters

○ Register for preschool(s) (additional research on preschools can be done later—see Chapter 4)

○ Babyproofing

○ TIPS AND SUGGESTIONS

○ REFERENCE INFORMATION

Chapter Two

FOUR MONTHS TO ONE YEAR—
ADAPTING TO NEW PRIORITIES,
ROLES, AND ROUTINES

At this time, the newness of motherhood may begin to feel less overwhelming. You may be thinking about your life as you go forward with your new baby. You can be sure it will be different, whether you are at home full-time with your baby, are working part-time, or are working full-time.

If you had a career and were employed before becoming a mother, your prior normal life had a routine with specific beginnings and ends to the tasks and jobs for which you were responsible. You interacted and had conversations with adults. You received recognition and payment for the time and effort you invested in your job and career. That life is gone.

This is particularly true if you are staying at home full-time with your baby. Your life will have changed to an immediate and singular focus: your baby. You will be on your own, taking care of your infant. Regular interactions and conversations with other adults will be scarce. Your compensation will be the smiles your baby gives you and knowing you are doing your best to nurture and care for your baby each day.

If you have gone back to employment part-time or full-time, your focus will have changed also. You'll be looking for an ideal balance of quality and flexibility for your infant's care. Your baby's adaptability and comfort with the people and the environment where she is being cared for is important. So too is the cost of childcare. Finding this balance for you, your baby, and your family is complex.

Your job, career path, and income potential will each be factors to consider. You may be able to set up a flexible schedule with your employer that allows you to continue on your career path. *See Box: Employment Flexibility Considerations.* An ideal balance does not mean a perfect balance. It means it is the best acceptable solution that is currently manageable and available. Know changes can always be made down the road.

Many studies have been done about the differing benefits to children of being raised by mothers who are employed full-time or part-time, or mothers who stay at home full-time with their children. These studies have been analyzed in numerous articles and books. I have read many of them. Since there is no consensus as to the best way for mothers to approach employment or staying at home in order to provide ideal conditions for their children, try to find a balance that makes you happy. Ultimately, your baby will benefit if you are happy. Where and how you find balance will change based on your priorities, needs, family demands, responsibilities, the workplace, the economy, and many other factors. There isn't a right or wrong answer to how you manage your circumstances.

EMPLOYMENT FLEXIBILITY CONCERNS

O One avenue to employment flexibility is to negotiate your schedule with your employer. This may help you find balance. Pursue an arrangement that will benefit both you and your employer.

O You might propose creating a job share role within your company where you and a coworker split days in the office. You might consider working longer hours, four days a week so you could have three-day weekends.

O Many companies are willing to structure job responsibilities to give parents the flexibility they need while raising their children. They realize without flexibility, many workers (mothers especially) will end up leaving. Companies would prefer not to lose experienced workers and then have to incur the disruption and additional costs required to train replacement workers.

O See Chapter Nine Resources, for Chapter Two, Mothers, Employment, and Career Navigation— Reading: Articles and Books.

If you do go back to employment, you'll be apt to wrap up your job responsibilities quickly and efficiently so you can pick Baby up from day care on time or get home to relieve your babysitter or nanny. Your low-grade anxiety and worry about your baby will dissipate once you are reunited. Part two of your day will then be underway: preparing and eating dinner with your spouse or partner, caring and connecting with Baby, and being together as a family.

Before you were a mother, you probably understood your role, occupation, or profession and its related requirements. This was true in my case. I was a student for many years, a college graduate, and then a businesswoman pursuing a meaningful career. As a student, I went to class and studied hard; after graduation, my career required training, development, getting to work on time each day, and taking care of business. The paths were clear. To reach many goals, the steps we need to take are straightforward. Our success is determined by how well we follow the rules, how hard we work, study, train, or practice.

The path of motherhood, however, is not clear, straight, or smooth. Think of it as a journey you are taking by boat on a long and winding river. The river is beautiful, but it is a force of nature. You will be subject to the weather, prevailing winds, the bends and turns of the riverbed, and unseen elements beneath the water's surface. Some days the river will be calm. You'll have blue skies with sunshine overhead, bathing you in the warmth of pleasant temperature. Your journey will be a delight—idyllic. Other days will be rough, and you'll be tossed about on choppy waves brought on by a storm. Pitching against the wind, you'll flounder while battling to get back to smoother water and a more peaceful journey.

Each day you will do your best. Know that you don't need to do every single thing perfectly. Appreciate that you are going through on-the-job training and learning as you go. The main thing to realize is you will accomplish what needs to be done. Your baby will get fed, you will get fed, and you both will get *some* sleep. Tomorrow, you will have time again to contemplate this new world of motherhood and how to cope with and enjoy it. Meanwhile, you'll wake up with a bit more skill and ability, which you have gained through today's on-the-job training.

You will begin to see the world from your baby's viewpoint and to discover new aspects of being a mother. When Baby is an infant, you may not have thought of her as being her own person, because she is not yet able to put her feelings and thoughts into words.

My mother would often say, "Babies are people." This is, of course, true. Like all people, your baby craves sociability.

Babies crave sociability. Talk to and listen to your baby.

So talk to Baby about how you are learning; tell her about what you will be doing that day and about your ideas and thoughts. See how she reacts to your voice, looks at you, and responds in her own way.

Talking to Baby develops her confidence, knowing that when she cries, you will comfort her. She senses the sympathy in your tone and feels reassured. She absorbs your empathy, which down the road will make her sensitive and responsive to others. She will delight you with her smiles, laughs, animated gestures, and amusing baby motions. Coax out her playfulness by playing peek-a-boo, this little piggy, the wheels on the bus, and other games; blow on her tummy, make funny faces, and giggle together. Notice how you enjoy each other and have fun together. These are some of the sweet joys of motherhood.

POSTPARTUM DEPRESSION

Review the following guide from the website webmd.com to learn more about its symptoms and treatments:

Postpartum Depression Guide (https://www.webmd.com/depression/postpartum-depression/understanding-postpartum-depression-basics#1)

It's important to know that it is normal for your days to not yet feel routine. You have never done this before. If you are at home with your baby full-time, this is an entirely new experience being responsible twenty-four hours a day, seven days a week for everything another human being needs. Of course, you love your wonderful new baby, but adapting to the extreme change in your daily life takes time. Recognize this and be patient with yourself and your baby. You and your baby are new to this.

Again, as mentioned in *Chapter One*, many mothers get the baby blues within the first few days following birth, ending within two weeks after birth. However, if you are still overwhelmed, or feeling hopeless or depressed, talk with your doctor about your symptoms. You may have postpartum depression and need treatment for this condition. *See Box: Postpartum Depression.*

Plan an outing with Baby every day.

If your day is spent entirely with your baby, have a destination or an activity that will get you out of your apartment or home each day. To go out for a couple of hours, you'll need to plan ahead. You want Baby to be content so your outing is successful. If she is not happy, she'll let you know. You may be in a place where you can't attend to her immediate needs. Her crying may increase its urgency, sending jolts of stress through your veins and the message that you need to abandon your plans immediately to comfort her.

I had this experience early on with my daughter. I took her in the Baby Bjorn carrier to run errands for a couple of hours, thinking she'd be fine. We'd barely reached the store when she began to fuss. I had underestimated when she'd need to nurse again and couldn't find a suitable spot to feed her. With her fussing growing louder, I ran outside to hail a taxi to go home. As we drove uptown, my daughter's cries turned to screams, agitating the cab driver. He sped uptown, weaving in and out of traffic to get us home and out of his cab ASAP. That was very stressful! Unfortunately, these sorts of problematic outings will occur from time to time, despite your best efforts to prevent them.

To avoid them, plan ahead; think about when Baby is at her best. For my daughter, this was after her morning or afternoon nap. As soon as she woke from her nap, I would feed and change her and then leave immediately. To do so, I needed to be completely ready along with her fully stocked diaper bag before she woke. *See Box: Diaper Bag Tips.*

When you are out, you'll find people will often stop you to ask, "How old is your baby?" Women will want to talk to your baby and tell you how cute she is or tell you a story about their baby and then inevitably say something like, "Enjoy them now. They grow up so quickly," or, "They don't stay young for long." Sometimes I felt impatient with people saying this all the time. In retrospect, I think they were just

DIAPER BAG TIPS

○ Restock and supply your baby's diaper bag with the essentials each evening. This can be the last thing you do each night before bed.

○ Add any additional items needed for tomorrow. Place it by the door, ready to go. This will smooth your departure each morning.

trying to be friendly and more than likely recalling fond memories of their own babies at that age. Perhaps we all may find ourselves saying or thinking the same thing, further down the road.

Most of the time, Baby will enjoy the attention of strangers. She'll kick and flail her legs and arms, with her eyes focused on her admirer. She might smile, opening her mouth as if to speak, showing her pleasure at meeting this new person. It's no wonder everyone loves babies. Occasionally, you'll meet someone who wants to get too close to your baby or may inadvertently make her cry. Maybe the person looks strange, smells funny, or your baby is already overwhelmed and is feeling hungry or tired. Don't worry; this shouldn't make you or the stranger feel embarrassed. Some babies' temperaments just make them more sensitive than others, and they are less comfortable engaging with unknown people. Simply saying, "My baby is feeling a bit overwhelmed today" can subtly dissuade people from approaching. If your child has a striking characteristic such as very curly hair that draws people to want to touch it, you are entirely right in saying,

"Please do not touch my child." If a stranger wants to take a picture of your child, usually he or she will ask your permission. It is entirely up to you to decide if you want to allow that person to do so.

When you first brought Baby home, you didn't have the time or the need to socialize. Your mom or your spouse's or partner's mom was with you to help out. And other relatives and friends stopped by to meet the new baby. Just getting your baby fed and changed and trying to get out for a bit of air each day was a challenge. Now, if you have gone back to being employed, you've had even more of a challenge—getting acclimated to a new schedule that involves taking care of your baby in the morning, possibly getting her to day care, and then rushing off to your job.

Having people with whom you can share your new priorities, questions, and experiences is important. Look for connections with other mothers, whether you are home full-time with your baby or employed. Your friends from pre-motherhood days will probably not realize the amount of energy you must expend to take care of your baby. I know that before I had children, I had no idea that babies need all-consuming energy and attention.

My sister had children before I did, and I had been used to having long conversations with her. Once her baby arrived, we could no longer have leisurely talks; our conversations would be short and end abruptly. I felt annoyed and impatient, and I didn't understand why she couldn't talk to me while taking care of her baby. Now I realize that expecting her to do so was unreasonable. We can't automatically assume that our close friends—or even our siblings—who don't have children will

CONNECT WITH MOMS

○ Mothers' Organizations (www.karenbongiorno.com
/it-takes-a-village)See resources under It Takes a
Village.

○ You can also use the following terms to search online
for ways to connect with other mothers:

- Mothers' Clubs/groups)
- employed mothers' baby playgroups
- Meetup mothers
- your town; mothers' groups
- new mothers' groups

be understanding or supportive in the way we need them to be once we are mothers.

As you begin to feel more capable, look for ways to connect with other mothers whose children are in the same age range as yours. You will want a peer group of mothers. They will be invaluable for support and for sharing information, stories, and friendship. Research groups oriented to new mothers in your area. Looking online is an excellent place to search. *See Box: Connect with Moms.* You'll find a number of mothers' organization websites that can help you find a group near you or give you information on starting your own group. You can also ask for referrals and suggestions from your pediatrician, obstetrician, and the hospital where your baby was born. Talk with the mothers you met in your Lamaze or other pre-baby classes.

Look for community activities oriented to new mothers

and babies. Your local recreation department, places of worship, or the YMCA may host classes for mothers and their young babies. Consider going to a weekly "mommy and me" class, where mothers play side by side with their babies. The classes provide a low-key stimulus for your baby and also allow you to meet other mothers in your neighborhood. Try various activities to see which experiences suit you and your baby. Some you will like; others you may not. You'll discover what kind of classes and places you enjoy.

It's easy to become isolated as a new mother, especially if your friends and neighbors are not mothers. So arrange to meet and plan activities and outings with other mothers and babies. It can be as simple as meeting at a coffee shop or at one another's home, talking for an hour while your babies play next to you on a floor mat. Or you might join a local Mothers' Club to be in a playgroup. (*See Chapter Three for more information on Mothers' Clubs.*)

Whether you are employed or stay at home, find a group or organization of mothers with whom you can spend regular time. Don't hesitate to reach out to mothers you see at the playground, library, day care, your job, grocery store, or in the neighborhood. If your place of employment has an internal newsletter, consider "advertising" in it to connect with other mothers. Or ask your town recreation department to put a notice on their website to attract members to begin and/or join a mothers' and babies' group.

If you are a stay-at-home mom with a spouse or partner, you'll have two parts to your day: part one, when you are mostly on your own, taking care of your baby; and part two, when your spouse or partner gets home to help. He or she will bring you the relief of a sympathetic ear, someone to talk with, to help you and give you a sweet moment of personal time. In turn, your partner will want relief from the workday and time to unwind. Since you will both be seeking a chance to unwind and "de-stress" at the same time, this is a dilemma.

You and your spouse or partner may both be employed full-time or part-time, one of you may be employed full-time and the other part-time, or one of you may be employed full-time while the other is at home full-time. With a baby in the house, it's not possible to take a break to unwind. "Babies are constant," my mom would say, a reminder that babies don't have a pause button to press that would give you time to relax.

Figuring out how to jointly divide the evening tasks and routines when you are both tired is important and will most likely involve compromise. You'll spend most of your evenings preparing dinner and then cleaning up, playing with and reading to your baby, as well as taking care of her bedtime and other nightly routines. When she is finally asleep, you'll have a brief period to relax and catch up with your spouse or partner before it's time for bed.

Trial and error will determine which responsibilities each of you prefers to handle. You will learn to notice when each of you is overwhelmed or has reached his or her limit, jump in, and take responsibility. Maybe your baby has been fussy all day, and when your spouse or partner gets home, you need

> Share tasks and responsibilities with your spouse/partner.

him or her to take over immediately so you can finally use the bathroom and get relief. Or maybe your partner's day was stressful, compounded by an extra-long drive home in horrible traffic. In that case, you'll need to get along without help. Maybe he or she can get down on the floor to play with your baby, who will be delighted. Your partner's spirits will feel revived by being immersed in her sweet and uncomplicated world.

If you are a single mother, you will not have the support and help of a partner at the end of your workday. This is difficult. You won't be able to get much-needed downtime until after your baby is asleep. Many mothers have spouses or partners who travel a lot for work or work long hours and aren't available to help with the evening and night routines. This makes for very long days.

Once your baby is asleep, use the time before you go to bed to relax. Do something you enjoy. You do not need to be productive. This is good advice

> Take time off from mommy-hood to feel rejuvenated.

for all mothers and fathers. Once your baby is asleep, relax. Having a baby in the house requires an enormous amount of energy. Avoid burnout by taking time to recharge.

Look for reliable babysitters to give you personal time and time out with your spouse or partner and other friends. In some communities, finding an affordable, reliable, and available babysitter is extremely difficult. You want to find someone trustworthy, someone able to handle your baby, and someone who doesn't charge too much. This was always a challenge for my husband and me. Asking friends to refer a babysitter was not always helpful either. A shortage of babysitters could mean friends hesitate to give you their babysitter's name, fearing you might book her when they need her. One possibility is to become a member of a babysitting co-op through a Mothers' Club or other organization. These can work if you are able to trade off, helping each other equally and at convenient times. The success of using a babysitting co-op can also depend on your baby's temperament and activity level.

If you are lucky enough to have a reliable babysitter, getting out for a date with your spouse or partner is always a welcome occasion. It's good to be together, just focusing on each other, away from parenting. Try to do this once a month. Assuming you are happy with your babysitter, and she is available (this can be difficult), you'll need to take into consideration your children's schedule(s) and temperaments to determine when you can be away, and for how long.

If your child's temperament makes it difficult for others to care for her, you'll need to keep your outings brief. This was the case for us. Getting out for a date was a rare occasion for my husband and me after our son arrived. As I mentioned earlier, he cried so much we didn't want to leave him for long. On one occasion, when our son was about five months old, we went out in the evening for dinner with friends who were on a rare visit from out of town. When we got home, our babysitter told us that our son had cried so much that she didn't want to babysit him ever again. I was mortified that my child had caused our babysitter to quit, but more than that, I was upset because I really needed a reliable babysitter to allow me a break from time to time. I called my sister to confess my embarrassment that our child had actually caused our babysitter to quit. She was completely sympathetic and assured me I should not feel embarrassed because babies *do* cry. I felt better but, at that point, it was true, our son did cry a lot, which made it, unfortunately, continually hard for us to get out.

Our experience is a good illustration of why you want to know that your babysitter is capable and comfortable with taking care of your baby or child, especially if your baby is challenging. You'll need to ensure that the babysitter you hire has the maturity and patience to handle those challenges. You don't want a babysitter to mistreat your child out of anger or frustration because she has become overly stressed by your child.

After our babysitter quit, we used Rent-a-Parent, an organization that connected us with mature and experienced babysitters. The cost for the babysitter would sometimes exceed the cost of our date, after adding the agency's fee to the cost of the four-hour minimum babysitting time.

Other avenues for finding babysitters: look through neighborhood websites, high schools, community colleges, and places of worship. Their organizations may have high school students who have signed up for after-school or part-time work. Inquire at your neighborhood elementary school, middle school, or nursery school about teachers who have an interest in babysitting.

Begin to learn about the choices for local preschools before your child is one. If there are a limited number of preschools in your area, you'll want to put her on one or two waiting lists to ensure she has a spot available when she is ready. Some preschools have an excess demand for enrollment, and you will need to put her on the school's waiting list before she turns one.

BABYPROOFING YOUR HOME

○ Learn what you need to do to make your home safe for your soon-to-be crawling, climbing, walking, curious, and active child.

○ Review baby and childproofing websites, books, or articles. You can buy gadgets, locks, covers, and pads and install them.

○ You can also hire "babyproofers" to bring, install, and arrange your home to make it safe for your child.

To find nearby preschools, ask for referrals from friends, your pediatrician, your obstetrician, and other mothers; also, go online. Contact two or three preschools to find out about admissions and how to enroll your child. It will be enough to register your child for now. You can begin to take tours and determine the specifics of what you want in the next couple of years. (*Chapter Four* has more information on choosing preschools.)

In the meantime, your baby will grow; her schedule and routines will change and vary. Time will pass, with no slow-downs to mark the milestones your baby will reach and pass on the way to being one year old. She will begin to turn over, lift herself up, and crawl, stand, maybe walk or climb. She'll smile and laugh, begin to babble, and form a few words or sounds. She'll enjoy playing with anything and everything. She will attempt to put everything in her mouth. She'll also have favorite toys, activities, and books. Her first teeth will come in. She will begin to eat solid foods and may stop breastfeeding. You might buy her first shoes. About the time she begins to crawl, you'll want to babyproof your home. *See Box: Babyproofing Your Home*. She is mobile and will need constant watching to keep her safe.

You'll be happy as you see her grow and reach these incremental milestones. Although exhaustion will still be with you, you will feel exhilaration and joy too. Your journey continues to progress and unfold. Keep going, dear Mother.

TIPS AND SUGGESTIONS—FOUR MONTHS TO ONE YEAR

+ New Tip or Suggestion
* Prior Tip or Suggestion to Continue

YOUR BABY'S WELL-BEING	+ Begin reading to your baby; show her the pictures. + Find "mommy and me" activities to go to with your baby. + Babyproof your home before your baby begins to crawl. + Screen time is not recommended for children under two years old by the American Academy of Pediatrics. * Put aside your phone and electronics when nursing or feeding your baby and during one-on-one time. * Talk to your baby.
YOUR WELL-BEING	+ Set aside time each day, even if it is brief, to give yourself a break. Establish a meaningful ritual for this time. + Arrange with your spouse, partner, or caregiver to care for your child at a regular time each week to give you time for personal restoration. Do something you enjoy (no tasks). * Buy cozy, attractive pajamas so you can feel "halfway attractive," while the other half of you feels like a zombie during the long nights of caring for your newborn. * Don't try to get back into your pre-pregnancy clothes yet. * Buy clothes for nursing (if you are breastfeeding). * Be patient with yourself. It is enough for you to feed and take care of your baby and yourself each day.
FAMILY	* Look for reliable babysitters.

(continued on next page) ▶

▶ *(continued from previous page)*

YOUR VILLAGE/ COMMUNITY	+ Learn about community organizations for mothers/families. + Consider starting or joining a playgroup. + Meet your neighbors.
PRESCHOOL	+ Find out how soon children need to be registered for preschool in order to have an available spot when they are age three. + If you are in an area where preschools have limited availability, visit preschools and register your child or put her on a waiting list. (See Chapter Four for further discussion of preschools.)

REFERENCE INFORMATION—FOUR MONTHS TO ONE YEAR
☆ SAVE LONG-TERM

☆ **BABY'S IMMUNIZATION RECORDS**
Keep track of your baby's immunizations.
Go to: www.cdc.gov/vaccines/parents/downloads/mile stones-tracker.pdf for a printable immunization schedule.

☆ **BABY'S HEALTH RECORDS—NOTES**
Keep the notes you take at pediatrician and other health-care appointments.

☆ **IMPORTANT CONTACTS REFERENCE LIST**
Create a contact list to post in your home for babysitters and other caregivers: include doctors, caregivers, hospital, emergency phone numbers, relatives, neighbors.

☆ **COMMUNITY GROUP(S)' MEMBERSHIP DIRECTORY(S)**
(if any)

In Chapter Three:

AGE ONE

(your baby/child will be referred to as "he")

- Reflections on Baby's first year
- "It takes a village"—building a support network
  - Finding a mothers'/parents' club
  - Playgroups
  - Community groups and activities
- Raising your child—basic concepts
  - Know and understand your child
  - Pay attention to your instincts
  - Use common sense
  - Get answers/solutions from a trusted source
- Safety awareness
- Fulfilling responsibilities and setting priorities
  - Erractic schedule
  - Time for self, spouse/partner
- New roles
  - Advocate
  - Gather, investigate, vet information
  - Research
- Follow up with preschool(s) if necessary
- TIPS AND SUGGESTIONS
- REFERENCE INFORMATION

Chapter Three

AGE ONE—
BEGINNING COMMUNITY

Happy first birthday, Baby! Time to celebrate Baby's first year and a year of being a family! You will marvel at how you've grown together, how you've managed to navigate all the bumps, twists, and turns of motherhood and make it so far. You'll love how Baby has established himself at the heart of your family, how you are discovering his personality and what makes him happy, what makes him laugh, what he enjoys, and how much joy he's brought into your life.

In this one fast, blurry, erratic year, a strong and lasting love has grown within you. It developed during the days and long nights you spent nurturing your baby. You have taken care of Baby, clumsily at first, but then with rapidly increasing skill and confidence. You have protected and provided for your baby to reach this day. He has grown considerably, as have you. Congratulations on your first year of motherhood!

This is a happy occasion to share with your extended family and friends who share love for your dear, sweet, adorable one-year-old. Lighting his first birthday candle and seeing him taste his first birthday cake is somehow quite poignant. It is a very special birthday.

Although Baby will not remember this day, many details of this birthday will stay with you. You'll remember coming into his room first thing in the morning and feeling so happy to say, "Happy birthday!" You'll repeat this to him throughout the day. You'll want to keep the cute invitation you sent the guests for his party. You may frame it, to begin a collection of invitations marking each year. He'll taste his birthday cake, getting crumbs and frosting stuck on his face, and make you laugh. You'll remember how wonderful it was to share this celebration with your family and friends, and how they gathered to merge their voices in a loud and enthusiastic singing of "Happy Birthday." You'll remember how you felt, surrounded by love for Baby as everyone watched you help him blow out his one meaningful candle. Memories of this day will linger, like that candle flame, as a beautiful warm glow.

This is a good time to pause and reflect. Mothers, please do not wait to experience the joy of being a mom until you feel you know exactly what you are doing and that you have everything under control! If you do, you will be waiting a very long time, and your child may already have moved out of your home. Appreciate that bringing up your baby and child will not be perfect, but it will be full of adventure, learning, surprise, and so much joy.

Stay-at-home mothers, continue to get out of the house each day with your baby, and go places where you can meet other mothers. Employed mothers, plan to do this on weekends, or in the evening, if possible. Look for neighbors with families. Stop to chat and get to know them.

Before becoming a mother, I hadn't thought about the importance of support from a nurturing community. "It takes a whole village to raise a child." I like the friendliness embodied within this African proverb, which implies commitment and concern within one's community for each child's well-being. As mothers, we have an ongoing responsibility for our families. It makes sense to have friends who understand and organizations that support the work and demands we have as mothers. We do need a village to back us up and collaborate with us to raise our children in a nurturing and caring environment.

> "It takes a whole village to raise a child." This African proverb embodies the friendliness of a community caring for its children.

Over the years, you will create a network from your contacts and relationships that become your circle of support for you and your family. This will be your village. It will grow through your involvement and connections in your community, through your child's activities and schools, and through organizations you join.

Join an organization where you can feel involved and supported as a mother, if you haven't already done so. Look for a mothers' or parents' club in your area. Your town recreation department's website or office will usually have listings of local mothers' or parents' clubs. You can search online by zip code. Ask at your pediatrician's office, your OB/GYN's office, baby supply stores, or ask mothers you see at the park or elsewhere. Your community newspapers may also list neighborhood

* See Resources: Chapter Two, Connect with Moms (http://www.karenbongiorno.com/it-takes-a-village).

Mothers' Clubs. If none exist in your town, you can begin one through your town's recreation department. It will be a welcome addition to the community.*

When I became a mother, I didn't think about needing more friends, since I already had longtime friends, colleagues from work, and relatives around the country. I really had no idea how much I would appreciate meeting the new group of friends and families I found through the Mothers' Club and in our neighborhood. Our mutual support contributed so much to our lives.

One of the most important purposes of a Mothers' Club is to connect mothers through playgroups based on the age of members' babies. Ideally, the babies will have birthdays within four to six months of each other, and you will find a playgroup that works with your schedule. If you are an employed mother, you'll want a playgroup with other employed mothers. Stay-at-home mothers will want a group with other stay-at-home moms.

Once you have your group, start by determining a good day and time to meet each week. Employed mothers may want to meet on the weekend; stay-at-home mothers may prefer a weekday. Six mothers in a group is a good number because it allows for enough members to meet, even when absences and delays occur. As you know, when you're dealing with babies and children, it's easy for something to come up that keeps mothers from getting out of the house or to places on time. You can meet at local parks or go for stroller walks. Check out the parks in and around your neighborhood and begin your walks at varying places so you can explore new locations. When the weather is bad, meet at libraries, cafés, indoor playcenters, indoor malls, or rotate hosting playgroup in your homes.

When you first start with your playgroup, talk about the importance of coming to playgroup regularly. You want mothers to be dedicated to making it to playgroup as often as possible. As a first-time mom, being in a playgroup might be your only reliable connection to other mothers and babies, so you want to be able to count on these regular meetings. When your children are little, you may want to meet for short time periods and then lengthen your outings as they get older.

Playgroups are invaluable.

Occasionally, playgroups don't work well for a mom or her baby; the timing could be off, the day of the week no longer convenient, or the members are absent too much. It's best to try to resolve these difficulties by discussing them within your playgroup. If it's not possible to find a solution, see if you can join another established group or form a new group. Be patient while you search for the right fit.

You'll get to know the other mothers in your group quickly as you spend time together, comparing notes, asking and answering questions. Your personal experiences during pregnancy and delivery, breastfeeding, and thoughts and suggestions for handling numerous issues will all become natural topics to discuss. You'll find that your way of thinking might be changing too. For example, jokes dealing with the potty or other bodily functions that previously you would have found dreadful are now tolerable, perhaps even funny. You'll share many stories and learn from one another as you see how your children navigate each of their developmental stages.

Many playgroups will meet for years in one form or another until the children are in kindergarten. Others will lead to friendships among mothers that last into high school or beyond. There is something about sharing motherhood for the first time that leads to lasting friendships. You watch many of your children's "firsts" together, and you support one another by sharing your experiences and asking for advice. You get to know the other children in your group and their personalities. These children are your child's first playmates. You love these children.

Looking back at my own experience, joining the local Mothers' Club was one of the best things I did. I really had no idea how much I would appreciate meeting the new group of friends and families and how much our mutual support would contribute to our lives. We had moved our little family from New York City to the suburbs of San Francisco when our daughter was just four months old. We lived in temporary housing for four months while we searched for the right neighborhood and home. When we finally moved into our home, we were eager to put down roots and couldn't wait to meet people and begin life in our new community.

Happily, my sister Margaret and her family and another friend, Judi, and her family lived in neighboring towns. Both Margaret and Judi had children a few years older than our daughter. My sister had joined her local Mothers' Club and found new friends and a playgroup that she and her kids loved. She recommended that I look for a Mothers' Club near me.

Coincidentally, Judi had been active in forming a Mothers' Club in her community and was able to put me in touch with a new club that was just beginning in our neighborhood.

I called and spoke with the membership coordinator, Thana, who made me feel at ease immediately. She had a baby girl just a few months older than my daughter. Her pre-baby life, like mine, had been full-time employment in a professional career. She and her husband had also moved recently, cross-country, from New York City. Thana was now at home full-time with her baby, desperately seeking outside communication, support, and stimulus. I knew exactly what she meant and felt instantly connected to her.

Thana introduced me to the Mothers' Club playgroup coordinator to find an age-appropriate group for my daughter and me. Before long, I was part of a new playgroup of six mothers with similar-aged children. Among the six of us, we had three boys and three girls. Our group was made up of four first-time mothers and two second-round mothers. We had much to share. We met weekly, usually at a park, where our friendships began easily while we looked after our children. We got to know one another through our fragmented conversations that we'd carry on through starts and stops, often breaking off during mid-sentence to rescue, assist, or redirect our children as they played.

When Paula, Kristen, and I (all of us first-time mothers) discovered that our husbands traveled a lot, leaving us alone to care for our young children for many very long days, we began to share dinners at one another's homes or at child-friendly restaurants. These evenings together were fun for us and for our children. They were lifelines for getting us through the long days of single-parenting.

Our playgroup continued until our children began kindergarten. In the meantime, our group grew with new baby siblings: three boys and two girls. As our children got older, we began to hike and plan excursions to the zoo, the beach, the lake, children's museums, amusement parks, and more. Our playgroup was like most. We celebrated birthdays and a lot of holidays together. We loved each other's children and took pleasure at seeing their firsts just as much as seeing our own children's.

I still treasure the friends I made through our Mothers' Club and loved the time I was in the club. Going to meetings and events; getting to know mothers, children, and families in the surrounding neighborhoods; volunteering; and joining separate groups within our club was satisfying and made me feel a part of the community.

Beyond playgroups, you'll find much more to do and be involved with in a mothers' or parents' group or similar organization. *See Box, Mothers'/Parents'/Community Group Activities.* (These are examples from our Mothers' Club.) You can choose to participate as much or as little as you wish. You could join a group within the organization or even start your own group to share an interest such as hiking, reading, seeing movies, cooking, doing community outreach, and more. Your village will expand as you meet other members and families by attending events, participating in a shared interest group, or volunteering within the organization. Your village is so important; you need others who encourage and support you in what you are doing.

You are doing your best to nurture and raise your child while learning to interpret his needs, understand him, and best schedule his daily routines. You're learning his limits for playing, interacting, meeting new people, and going places.

MOTHERS'/PARENTS'/COMMUNITY GROUP ACTIVITIES

○ Groups
- Playgroups
- Book clubs
- Other

○ Social Activities
- Seasonal family parties
- New member gatherings
- Neighborhood brown bag lunch drop-ins
- Other

○ Parent Education
- Speaker series given by local experts
- Monthly newsletter written by members

○ Community Outreach
- Donation drives for local philanthropies

You'll have a lot to learn while raising your child, but much of the time you can rely on four basic concepts. *See Box on next page: Raising Your Child—Four Basic Concepts.* These begin with *knowing and understanding* (#1) your child. This develops your *instincts* (#2) for sensing the usual and normal range of your child's behavior. Pair these first two with *common sense* (#3), and you can be fairly certain that you are proceeding in the right direction. When you are unsure of what to do, despite your knowledge, instincts, and common sense, you'll know it's time to *look for answers or a solution* (#4).

RAISING YOUR CHILD—
FOUR BASIC CONCEPTS

1. Know and understand your child
2. Pay attention to your instincts
3. Use common sense
4. Get answers/solutions from a trusted source

You'll come to understand your child's natural tendencies as you learn his daily rhythms and patterns and the way he interacts and responds to people and his surroundings. If your child's behavior changes suddenly, hopefully your instincts will alert you to look for a reason. It took my daughter getting sick for the first time at six months old for me to learn to trust my instincts. My daughter had slept poorly, waking on and off, followed by being unusually cranky in the morning. I should have known that there was something wrong, but I didn't even consider that she could be sick, despite her uncharacteristic behavior. Her temperature showed that she didn't have a fever, but she was still uncommonly fussy after I fed and changed her. At that point, I didn't know what to think, so I called the pediatrician. She recommended bringing my daughter in to the office for a physical exam. It turned out my daughter had an ear infection and needed antibiotics. I could have avoided the delay in calling the pediatrician and bringing my daughter in for care if I had followed my instincts originally.

Research showing there are nine distinct temperament traits is helpful for understanding your child. It was done by Doctors Stella Chess, Alexander Thomas, and Herbert

THE NINE TEMPERAMENT TRAITS

1. Activity Level
2. Distractibility
3. Intensity
4. Regularity
5. Sensory Threshold

6. Approach/Withdrawal
7. Adaptability
8. Persistence
9. Mood

https://childdevelopmentinfo.com/child-development/
temperament_and_your_child/temp2/#.XL5GXS_MzfZ

Birch in the 1950s. It describes nine distinct temperament traits that each of us can have in varying degrees. These traits affect how we behave. *See Box: The Nine Temperament Traits.* You don't need to study these traits intensely, but the information is interesting and can be useful. Each trait can be measured at a high, moderate, or low level. There are no "good" or "bad" trait levels. Knowing the usual level your child's behavior places him at for each trait is a valuable component to understanding him.

You can identify your child's traits and corresponding levels by observing how he responds to meeting, playing, and interacting with you and with others, how he reacts in different situations and circumstances, and what is reasonable to expect from him. This knowledge can guide you in the way you manage his routines and transitions. When he gets older, this knowledge will help you teach him how to manage on his own. For now, you are learning Baby's limits for playing, interacting, meeting new people, and going places.

In the meantime, enjoy discovering what interests Baby and what sparks his imagination. You are seeing his unique personality emerge as he takes hold of you with his baby hands and pure heart.

Now, when your child is just beginning to walk, run, and climb, you'll need to watch for potential hazards your child can trip on, fall over, fall from, and bump into. At this age, your child is prone to getting hurt because he has not yet learned how to avoid unsafe situations, items, and behavior. Staying close to him at all times means you'll be able to dash to his rescue in an instant. You'll constantly be on your feet.

Some children will be more active than others, as was my son. He began to crawl at five months and then to walk at seven months. I was always running after him, yelling, "Danger!" No matter what he was doing, he would be in a hurry to do it or to get there; he'd pay no attention to steps, the coffee table, or toys strewn on the floor in front of him. He'd rush over and through them and then get hurt when he fell or tripped. At the playground, he would climb on the jungle gym, cross to the opposite side, and decide to step into the air from five feet up. I'd need to rush over to catch him, and in doing so I would get my own set of bruises and scrapes. One time on a very warm day, I heard him yelling from the top of a slide. In an instant, I realized that the hot metal slide must be burning his legs. I ran full speed up the slide to save him, without seeing the crossbar halfway up, because the cap I was wearing obscured it. The force of running into the crossbar knocked me backwards, but not before I pulled my son onto my lap so we could slide down safely. The raised black bump on my forehead was the price I paid for saving my son's tender skin from being seared that day.

Unfortunately, accidents do happen, and somewhere along the way your child may get hurt or injured, no matter how alert you are to danger or how thoroughly you have baby-proofed your home. This is heart-wrenching and stressful.

My son had his first incident requiring stitches when he was barely one year old. He tripped in the bathroom and split his chin open on a plastic wastebasket. (Who knew plastic could cut?) Seeing the tile floor slick and slippery from his blood was sickening. Although we used a warm, damp washcloth to apply pressure and stop the bleeding, it was obvious that he was going to need stitches to close the wound.

Naturally, his injury happened at night, when our pediatrician's office was closed. But my husband and I tried not to panic. We called Janet, our neighbor, to see if we could bring our daughter over to her house. "Of course," she said. We then drove our son straight to the emergency room. When we checked in at the ER, we were told to wait because the injury was not critical. Never wanting to sit still, our son was not happy to wait in one place, so he continued to cry loudly.

When a doctor was finally available, we took him in to be stitched up. His chin needed just a few stitches, but it took two male ER workers to hold him, still screaming, in a restrictive cocoon wrap so he wouldn't jerk and squirm while being stitched back together. Four hours after arriving at the ER, he was cleared to go home. The physician assured us that he would be just fine but was concerned that I was overly anxious and stressed. Given the long wait and hearing my son scream for close to four hours, my symptoms seemed normal. (Little did we know that visit was the first of five we would make to the ER over the years for our children's emergencies.)

You may have come to realize and understand that being a mother means you no longer have direct control of the way you spend your time and energy. Do not be discouraged by this, although it can be difficult to acknowledge. It took me a long time to learn this. I felt I should be accomplishing more. For

> Coming to terms with your responsibilities and setting your priorities and limits for what you can handle is a process.

some reason, I didn't recognize that I was being productive by taking care of my child! The days would come and go as most of my time was spent caring for my daughter. When she was awake, she needed almost complete attention, so I had limited time to do other tasks. Some days, I might complete some items on my to-do list; other days, none. I was often exhausted, and it seemed there was always enough still to be done to make me feel I was incompetent. It took me a long time to recognize that I was doing the best I could, and that was entirely sufficient.

If you are a stay-at-home mom, you'll be surrounded by necessary tasks that, in most cases, are uninteresting. At times, you may feel that what you are doing is insignificant, particularly compared to your recent career or whatever your education had prepared you for. Your to-dos will be simple: buy groceries; do laundry; run errands; handle bills, correspondence, and other deskwork; schedule appointments; and take care of the never-ending requirements for running a household. It's hard to find the motivation to do them all. Set small goals. Try working on something for fifteen minutes; see what you can get done in that short period. Later in the day, you may have another fifteen minutes to handle something else.

Caring for your baby will always come with disruptions to the plans you have for your day. Your baby's schedule will change just when you've become accustomed to it. His nap schedule might go from two naps a day to just one, throwing you off because you'd been using the time during his morning nap to get things done while you rest during his afternoon nap. You'll have to refigure when to rest and still manage your to-dos. On another day, you could be exhausted because your baby woke you on and off all night and needs to go to the doctor. You'll need to schedule an appointment with the pediatrician and cancel other activities. You probably wouldn't have much energy to do anything else anyway.

You'll have new common setbacks that upend your plans and extend the time it takes to get your errands accomplished. You could be delayed before you even get out because Baby decides to squirm about and hinder you buckling him into his car seat. Or, once you've arrived at your destination, he might decide to do the stiff-body move that keeps you from fastening him into his stroller. Weather is often a factor, making it complicated or even impossible to get out of the house. Delays are always frustrating, especially when you're strapped for time. Try to give yourself extra time when possible. It's no fun to feel rushed or harried.

You will have many routine things to do, as a mother, which you may not enjoy. Realize that most jobs, positions, or occupations, no matter their level of responsibility, creativity, or glamour, will include monotonous and repetitive tasks to produce the end product or outcome. The routine jobs you do are essential to maintaining your surroundings and to keeping your family on track. They set the tone in your home and help to provide a measure of harmony in your daily lives.

Taking care of your baby and keeping up with work and the household can be all-consuming, especially for mothers who are at home, part-time or full-time. It's important to make time for yourself. You need time to take your mind away from caring for your baby and your to-do list; you need time to just breathe so you can feel restored. This is vital to maintaining your sense of self and to avoid being depleted of energy. You are giving so much to your baby; you need nurturing too. Allow yourself some time each day to relax. Anything that lets you do so is beneficial. Meditate, listen to music, talk to a friend, garden, journal, read, take a walk, go for a run, or create a ritual to savor. Remember, you need to maintain your strength and vitality to have the energy to do a good job of taking care of your child.

If you are a part-time or full-time employed mom, you may have help doing some of these chores. (I hope you do!) You may be bothered less by these boring tasks because you don't see the mess or pile-up of things that need to be done throughout your entire day. The shift between being employed and coming home to take care of your child is quite a contrast. It's a tough transition. At your place of employment, you interact with your coworkers and carry out your responsibilities in a fairly systematic way. When you get home to your baby or child, you will be in the opposite kind of environment. You won't be able to handle your baby or child's needs in the professional and orderly way that you manage at work. Your baby will not be interested in waiting for you to unwind and transition into mommy-mode. He'll be happy to see and connect with you but will want to express his feelings and needs urgently. For employed mothers, it is equally important to find your own restorative time. Going back and forth between responsibilities can be very stressful and tedious.

For all mothers, be realistic in deciding what you are capable of doing. Let go of expectations for doing everything perfectly. This is easier said than done! Realize you don't have the time or energy to do so, and that is okay! Think instead about what is important to you; make those things your priority. Set limits where you can. Focus on the people and experiences in which you want to invest your precious time and spirit.

Along with taking time out for yourself, it's important to stay connected with your spouse or partner. The two of you need time to have fun together. Single moms, plan occasions to go out and enjoy yourself with friends. Being away from your child, employment, and responsibilities will refresh you and allow you to recharge, giving you a renewed spirit and fresh outlook.

There are other aspects of motherhood that come up that you might not have thought about but nonetheless become roles you take on. One of these is gathering and reviewing information. I hadn't realized how much information I would need to acquire and vet in order to make decisions for my children. Some decisions may require further research

> Decisions require information and sometimes additional research.

or an expert to educate you. Acting as advocate for your child is another role that you'll need to assume at times. For example, your child may have a pediatrician, doctor, or even a teacher or administrator who isn't able to treat a condition effectively or provide satisfactory answers to your questions or concerns. If you feel something is not right, trust your instincts and pursue

Sometimes you will need to advocate for your child.

the matter. Remember, your child cannot advocate for himself. In some cases, you may need to educate yourself in order to advocate responsibly. So, for example, if your child has a condition that needs treating, you will want to understand the condition and be assured he is receiving the best course of treatment. To educate yourself, you'll look for information. This research may lead you to pursue another avenue for answers or treatment in order to be able to advocate knowledgeably on your child's behalf.

I found myself in this position with my children on more than one occasion. In one example, my son (at an older age) was diagnosed with a condition that *could* be dangerous under some circumstances. The specialist doctor that we went to told us that the treatment course for our son would require a dramatic lifestyle change. My son, as well as my husband and I, were devastated at hearing this treatment that would impose restrictions on his activities. I vowed to research whether there were alternative ways to treat his condition. I learned about an approach that had just been proven effective in trials done at a top medical research institution. Further research led us to a local university doctor who was using this exact new method. We arranged a meeting with this doctor and went to see him with trepidation and cautious optimism. He turned out to be a brilliant and understanding doctor who took my son on and gave him a treatment plan that allowed him to resume his activities without any of the restrictive conditions prescribed by the previous doctor. Of course, we were extremely relieved. This was truly a worthwhile and fortunate outcome of research and advocacy.

Motherhood is a journey. You begin by carrying your child,

to keep him close and safe. You set him down with gentleness and within a safe perimeter. When he begins to crawl, you keep him from encountering rough or harsh surfaces. When he learns how to stand and climb, you install babyproofing gadgets and barriers to ensure his safety. When he begins to walk and run, you watch him constantly to keep him safe and rush to help him when he moves toward harm. You'll take on many roles that require varying skills and, at times, more time and patience than you may have. Organization will help, but your time will be limited each day. Continue to be flexible with your plans and reasonable with your expectations.

You will have good and bad days. When you are rested and feel energetic, you will have fun; the little games and activities you and your child play will be entertaining for both of you. When you are exhausted, the same activities will seem tiresome; you'll feel as though the days are creeping along at a snail's pace. These times will pass as your baby slowly grows and changes. But know that now—while you are caring for your baby, playing with him and feeding him—you are nurturing him. He is absorbing your attention as the building blocks that form his first layer of trust and belief in the world around him. Your care instills these with the elements of understanding, encouragement, devotion, and unconditional love. Each block is integral to constructing your child's lasting foundation of confidence and security.

You are of great influence in your child's life. You are irreplaceable to him! You do not need to be a perfect mother. You are the best mother for your child simply because you are his mother; you love him, care for him and, for your child, this is what matters. Remember this and take heart and strength from it.

TIPS AND SUGGESTIONS—AGE ONE
+ New Tip or Suggestion
✶ Prior Tip or Suggestion to Continue

YOUR BABY'S WELL-BEING	+ Playgroup play ✶ Continue reading to your baby; show him the pictures. ✶ Go to "mommy and me" activities. ✶ Be sure your home is babyproofed. ✶ Screen time is not recommended for children under two years old by the American Academy of Pediatrics. ✶ Put aside your phone and electronics when feeding your child and during one-on-one time. ✶ Talk to your child.
YOUR WELL-BEING	✶ Set aside time each day, even if it is brief, to give yourself a break. Establish a meaningful ritual for this time. ✶ Arrange with your spouse, partner, or caregiver to care for your child at a regular time each week to give you time for personal restoration. Do something you enjoy (no tasks). ✶ Be patient with yourself. It is enough for you to feed and take care of your child and yourself each day.
FAMILY	+ Explore your local community to find organizations, businesses, and parks that are geared to mother, child, and families. + Find child-friendly restaurants. + Look for reliable babysitters.
YOUR VILLAGE/ COMMUNITY	+ Join or start a playgroup—if you haven't already. + Socialize with your neighbors. Get to know/meet and schedule playdates with neighboring families.

(continued on next page) ▶

▶ *(continued from previous page)*

YOUR VILLAGE/ COMMUNITY	* Consider volunteering within a community organization. * Learn about and join a community organization for mothers/families. * Inquire/look for playgroups in your neighborhood. * Meet your neighbors.
PRESCHOOL	+ Register your child for preschool. As I mentioned in the last chapter, if you are in an area where preschools have limited availability, visit preschools and register your child or put him on a waiting list. (See Chapter Four for further discussion of preschools.)

REFERENCE INFORMATION—ONE YEAR
☆ SAVE LONG-TERM

☆ **BABY'S IMMUNIZATION RECORDS**
Keep track of your baby's immunizations.
Go to: www.cdc.gov/vaccines/parents/downloads/mile stones-tracker.pdf for a printable immunization schedule.

☆ **BABY'S HEALTH RECORDS—NOTES**
Keep the notes you take at pediatrician and other health-care appointments.

☆ **IMPORTANT CONTACTS REFERENCE LIST**
Create a contact list to post in your home for babysitters and other caregivers: include doctors, caregivers, hospital, emergency phone numbers, relatives, neighbors.

☆ **COMMUNITY GROUP(S)' MEMBERSHIP DIRECTORY(S)**
(if any)

Chapter Four

AGES TWO AND THREE— EARLY CHILDHOOD

These years are the heart of early childhood. Your child will be extremely active and may need almost constant attention. This means that when you are with her, you'll need to stay close to her, watching to keep her from accidental injury while simultaneously keeping her busy and actively engaged. She will be fascinated by anything and everything! If you are a part-time or full-time stay-at-home mother, your days will have periods of time with no specific structure. Building routines and structure into your days will make it easier for you to handle the demands you face each day. Children at this age like routines, which makes them easier to implement. If you are an employed mother, build in routines for evenings and weekends.

Your child is beginning to learn how to be social, make decisions, make choices, and understand the concept of "mine." She has been talking, is actively learning new words, and is even beginning to talk in brief sentences. By the time

GESELL INSTITUTE STUDIES

○ There are individual books for ages one through nine. Each is titled by age, e.g., *Your One-Year-Old*, *Your Two-Year-Old*, etc.

○ The Gesell Institute was founded in 1950 and has been dedicated to understanding children's growth and how it affects development.

○ For more information, go to: www.gesellinstitute.org/

she is three, she may be able to communicate with, and be understood by, most people. She will begin to think about other children's feelings. She will enjoy routines and rituals but will continue to be easily distracted.

Part of understanding your child: As a mother, you'll read books, articles, and publications about raising children. Not all of the information you read will apply to your child, but you might gain insight into your child's behavior and ways to manage it. The book *Your Three-Year-Old*, one in a series written by Louise Bates Ames and Carol Chase Haber of the Gesell Institute of Human Development, was particularly helpful to me. *See Box: Gesell Institute Studies.*

The authors describe how children's behavior during this age will cycle in approximate six-month intervals. Their research found that children go through periods of being in and out of sync or equilibrium. This affects how children handle everyday routines and interactions. When a child is in sync, routines and interactions are easy, and she feels content. When a child is out of sync, everyday routines and interactions are difficult, and she feels out of sorts. A child's natural growth is responsible for these phases, particularly when the child is attempting to master new skills.

I was extremely relieved to learn about these cycles. I had been enjoying my daughter and how easily she interacted with others. Then, at about age three, she began to be quite difficult. I wondered what I

> Your child's behavior will cycle through a range of easy to challenging phases during these years.

was doing wrong and worried that struggling with my daughter would become a daily occurrence. Understanding that she was out of sync because she was going through a tough phase helped me get through this time. Both my children, in fact, went through these smooth and bumpy periods. Sometimes it was challenging, but I was encouraged, knowing that my children were behaving normally and that the rough patches would eventually level out.

Difficult phases will be evident when your child begins to resist former routines and simple requests, and "no" becomes her favorite word. Invariably, when you are ready to go somewhere, she'll dawdle and take "forever" to get into her clothes, use the bathroom, or find her shoes. Mealtimes will be a struggle because foods she used to eat have become unappealing. Completing routine tasks with her will be demanding and exhausting. You may find it easier to slow down during this period, allowing more time to get places and to accomplish things. My phrase for allowing the time to deal with a delay or issue, when it occurred, was "working it through." If I attempted to ignore the issue, or rush, it would require more effort and take longer to achieve. As an example, if your child really wants to button her own sweater, don't do it for her simply because you can do it faster; instead, allow time for her to do it. She will master new skills by practicing and by working through her frustrations. She'll become more adept and confident in her own ability, putting her on the path toward synchronization again.

During these years before your child begins formal schooling, you will have the flexibility to travel when you want. You won't need to plan around the annual school schedule, beginning in mid- to late August and lasting through mid-June. Take advantage of being able to go places, visit out-of-town relatives, and take family vacations without having to check for conflicts with school, sports teams, recitals, practices, and other seasonal activities, all of which begin to take precedence once your child begins kindergarten. An added advantage is that travel during the off-peak season means vacation spots are less crowded and rates are more reasonable.

> You can travel freely during these years because you don't yet have the restrictions of a school calendar and schedule.

It's terrific for your child to spend time with grandparents, cousins, and extended family. It allows her to get to know them, connect to her heritage, and see the continuity of family through the generations. Belonging to a family comes without demands or conditions. These relationships can be important, stabilizing bonds as your child grows older. Families, including cousins, grandparents, aunts, and uncles, have a mix of personalities, lifestyles, and ages. They will enrich your child's life with their presence. She'll see that people vary in their outlooks, relationships, and interactions, expanding the ways she thinks about and views the world.

I was happy that we spent as much time as we did with relatives in my children's early years. It was easy for grandparents to come for visits then, and to host us before we became busy with school and extracurricular activities. Our children were lucky to spend time with their many cousins who lived within a few hours' drive. The cousins kept up their friendships over the years, thanks to annual family reunions at Thanksgiving and other holidays, birthday celebrations, and graduation parties which took place as each cousin graduated from middle school, high school, and now, college.

Use this time to determine which preschool you would like your child to attend. If you had previously registered with preschools in order to have a spot for your child, visit and evaluate them. (*See Chapter Two, reserving a place in preschool for your child.*) You may decide to expand your search to other preschools because you have new information, referrals, or other requirements.

When you take tours of the schools you are considering, compare differences in the facilities, both indoors and outdoors. Observe how the teachers engage with the children and encourage the children to play with one another. Notice the kinds of activities in which the children participate. Find out how experienced the teachers and staff are and ascertain their ability to provide support to your child, and to you and your family. *See Box: Preschool Considerations.* Ask them the reasons and philosophy behind the schedule and activities for the children at their school.

PRESCHOOL CONSIDERATIONS

O A well-established preschool will generally have experienced teachers who can be tremendously helpful in answering questions or concerns you have about your child. If there is an issue to deal with, the teachers will be able to assist you in handling it.

O Seasoned teachers can also assure you when a concern you have is simply typical of the stage your child is going through, thereby relieving your worry.

Other points you might consider: Does the school facilitate parent socializing? Are parents encouraged to be in the classroom? Are there parent education speakers? School fundraising? Tuition assistance? Consider the school's location and the number of days and hours your child can attend. Preschools will set the number of hours children can attend, often just two or three days each week, according to the child's age. Some schools have aftercare hours that extend the time your child can be there.

Decide the characteristics that are important to you for your child's preschool. What kind of environment do you prefer, and will it be a good fit for your child? When you have made your choice or choices, be sure to register your child or place her on a waiting list at the school. If your child is wait-listed, check back with the school every few months to see if she is moving up the list. Be sure to sign up for an available and acceptable alternative school.

TYPES OF PRESCHOOLS

○ Go to: Preschool Philosophies
(https://www.greatschools.org/gk/?s=types%20
of%20preschools)
○ You'll find details of seven types of preschools and
explanations on how each type implements its
approach to child development and learning.

For more information on choosing a preschool, go online to see information on specific kinds of preschools, e.g., Waldorf, Montessori, Reggio Emilia. *See Box: Types of Preschools.* Many preschools will combine elements of each type of approach. You can do further research on ones you find appealing. You may not have a variety of schools in your area. However, learning about the various approaches is informative and gives you a frame of reference.

Think about what makes sense for your child and whether you are drawn to a particular style based on your personal values or philosophy. You want it to be fun and enjoyable for your child. The best way to gather information and impressions for making your decision is to visit the preschool and talk with the teachers and parents. Preschool should be a fun time while preparing your child gently for kindergarten and sociability. Recently, some preschools have changed their curriculum to a more academic model, rather than play oriented. The idea behind this is that children in these programs will do better academically once they are in school. Research has shown that the opposite occurs. *See Box: Preschool Research.*

PRESCHOOL RESEARCH

Go to the website challengesuccess.org and download the Preschool PDF shown under resources/research/do-you-know/

Around this time, when your child is becoming slightly less dependent, you may decide to add another child to your family. Being pregnant will be tiring, whether you are at home caring for your first child or going to work. Try to cut back on your activities, especially if you have to deal with morning sickness or physical stress. Adjust your schedule to give yourself quick breaks to put your feet up or to take a brief catnap. If you are at home, nap when your toddler naps, even if just for a short time. If you are too tired or nauseous to move about, lie on the floor or couch next to your child while she plays. I had to do this many times to survive long days and bouts of nausea when I was pregnant with my second child. If you are at work, put your feet up and find a quiet place to close your eyes during your lunch hour.

Be equally attentive, as you were with your first pregnancy, to caring for yourself. Eating healthily and going to all your pregnancy checkups will help ensure the health of your baby-to-be, as well as your own.

Once your new baby arrives, your family dynamics will change again. Your time will be occupied almost constantly with your new baby and his schedule, even while you are still managing your first child's needs and activities. Inevitably, your life will now be dominated by your children.

The good news is that you have become adept at handling the numerous small routines, equipment, and gear that go with babies. Changing diapers, bathing your baby, recognizing a fever, putting the stroller up and down, getting your baby in and out of the car seat, and strapping him into the Baby Bjorn are all skills you have mastered and can feel competent in handling. But you'll have times when you feel as though you are a sleep-deprived zombie, trying to satisfy the multiple demands of caring for your new baby, your first child, and also regular, everyday life.

When you bring your newborn home, you won't be able to predict how your older child will respond to her new sibling. She may be fascinated by this new little person who just arrived in the house and is getting so much attention. She may not be happy to have a new little sister or brother. It's best not to leave a child alone with a newborn. She could become jealous and want to harm the new baby. You'll need to teach your child how to play safely with her new brother or sister. As an example, your child might hurt your newborn accidentally by hitting or bumping him with a toy that could easily bruise or cut the baby.

My second child (my son) was born when my daughter was almost seventeen months. We learned quickly that she needed to understand how to be careful around her new baby brother. We would say, "Gentle!" each time she got near him. Her "pat" on his head was more like a bonk, and with greater impact than we thought she was capable of. She "hugged" him by lying on top of him. We showed her how to touch him softly and explained that playing next to him was the right way to play together. We wrote new words for a picture book with a young girl and infant brother, creating our own story about a wonderful big sister who played very carefully with her baby brother. We read it to our daughter many times. To be safe, we never left her alone with her infant brother.

I was thrilled to see that my daughter loved her baby brother, even though his arrival meant less attention for her. His eating, crying, squirming, and sleeping didn't directly involve her, yet she always wanted to be with him and to hold him. She was completely enthralled by him. If she couldn't hold him, she would squeeze close to him, the better to hug and kiss him. I found this very endearing! Fast-forwarding to the future, I hoped this emotional connection meant that my children would be good friends, enjoy one another growing up, and remain friends after they were grown.

If you have a child who doesn't appreciate her new baby sister or brother, involve or talk with her about the baby's care, to give her an understanding of what babies need. You could tell her about what you did for her as a baby, and how she grew out of her baby stages bit by bit. Depending on your first child's age, you could give her small jobs to help you with the baby. Perhaps she could get out a diaper, hand you baby wipes, or help pick out an outfit for the baby. You can find more tips for helping your child adjust to a new baby by going online.

When your first baby arrived, your social life changed. This change is multiplied when you have another child because you now have an additional schedule to work around. Your new baby needs to be fed and changed often, and he has his own nap schedule. You now have two children to bathe and get to bed each night. It's tricky and difficult, trying to take care of two children at the same time.

When we first became parents, we included our infant daughter in most of our outings and felt we had adjusted well to being parents. We didn't go to movies or fancy dinners, but we still went to restaurants, where she was happy to sit in her infant seat and later in a high chair, and to entertain herself by looking around at the other diners. Inevitably, when we were out, someone would stop by our table to talk to her and be delighted by her smiles. We even ventured out when she was about eleven months old on a weekend getaway to explore a quiet town's charming boutiques and restaurants. We strolled in and out of shops, enjoyed leisurely dinners, and had a lovely time. But it was a different story altogether when we went back to the same quiet town with both of our young children. We were met with unfriendly looks and stares. Sadly, it was not the same pleasant experience.

We realized that our outings and lifestyle needed to change further. First, there was an added schedule to consider. Next, we learned that we needed to account for our second

> A second child will naturally bring additional lifestyle changes.

child's temperament—how adaptable or amenable he was about going places and being content. We had not realized how "easy" our daughter (our first child) made it for us. She began sleeping through the night at exactly three months, took regular naps in the morning and afternoon, went to bed at a regular time, accompanied us on errands, traveled with us by car or plane, slept in hotels, at grandparents', and at other relatives' homes, all with a happy disposition and hardly a complaint. We secretly congratulated ourselves on being such capable parents. When our son arrived, our "impressive parenting skills" disappeared overnight. It turns out we had just been lucky that our first child's disposition made her an easygoing and good-natured baby.

Our second child had to be induced, two weeks after his due date. We imagined he was not happy to have been brought into the world before he was ready, so he made sure we knew this for the next six months by crying almost constantly when he was awake for eighteen to twenty hours a day. (Of course, being induced doesn't mean a baby will be colicky. In our son's case, our pediatrician couldn't find any specific reasons for his crying, although at one point she said, "He just doesn't like being a baby." This just seemed sad and was certainly not helpful.)

For me, it was a tough situation. I couldn't understand what I should be doing or why my baby wasn't happy. He would stop crying when he was nursing or being held, swinging in his swing seat, or if he had slept for a couple of hours earlier. Getting him to sleep at night was an ordeal, however. I tried using the Ferber method, which recommended letting your child cry himself to sleep. (Dr. Ferber claimed that babies would adapt and fall asleep through "self-soothing" after being allowed to cry for increasingly longer periods of time each night.) This method was stressful because hearing our son's crying made us feel miserable. Each night, though, he only slept a few hours. I lost track of how often I got up each night to soothe him. I would stay in his room, holding him until he fell asleep. Often, I tried to put him back in his crib, but he would wake again and cry. I became seriously sleep-deprived, but there was no time for me to nap during the day, with both children needing constant attention.

Later, when my son was older, we learned that Ferber had renounced his method. I was extremely angry to have followed his guidelines that had seemed so contrary to common sense. This is a good lesson as to why it's important to trust your own instincts as a mother. This way you will recognize when a particular course of action isn't effective for your child and be prompted to look for a better way to address her needs.

I was often on my own during that very stressful time because my husband's work required that he travel often, many times overseas, and for as long as two weeks at a time. I certainly learned from this experience to have empathy and understanding for the strain single parents go through, having to care for their children on their own.

One day I became completely overwhelmed. My son was crying while I was trying to get lunch ready in the kitchen. Our two cats, who had been with us since before our daughter was born, had become increasingly agitated since our son arrived. His constant crying, coupled with the lack of attention they were receiving, understandably made them anxious. They would follow me, meowing for attention, even when I went into the bathroom. I remember thinking, *Can't I have peace just for a minute?!* My cats' meowing was just another reminder that I wasn't even satisfying my pets. The cats would skulk through the house, their ears flattened, their eyes wild with the desire to escape the sound of my son's continuous crying.

That day, one cat climbed into the baby carriage and relieved himself on the fabric lining and blanket. That did it. I couldn't handle any more; I burst out crying. I shut the windows and patio door so the neighbors wouldn't hear me sobbing, and I gave in to my exhaustion and frustration. I didn't want to alarm my daughter, so I wiped my tears quickly. Crying did relieve some of my tension, but I understood that something needed to change. My husband agreed.

I wasn't used to not being able to handle my responsibilities, but I realized I needed help and more rest. I wasn't used to *needing* help; usually I *volunteered to* help. I wasn't sure what to do. Could I eliminate any unnecessary daily routines or jobs? I felt as if I were doing the minimum, as it was. Dirty clothes still needed washing; we still needed to eat. Could I do laundry less frequently? Get take-out meals? Call a friend to help me? No, my friends all had their own children to take care of. Maybe I could hire a nanny part-time, but it would have to be someone who was patient and mature enough to tolerate my son's crying.

Eventually, I found a nanny. Actually, our nanny found me. She saw us at a park that we went to frequently and asked me if I needed help. Yes, yes, I did! I was so thankful to have her work for us. She was able to come twice a week, for three or four hours at a time. She worked for another family already but wanted to work a few more hours each week. This was enough for me to get out of the house to run errands, rest, or focus on being with just one child. She worked for us for three years. About the time my son was one, I hired a house cleaner who came every other week. Gradually, our lives became a bit more manageable. I was still sleep-deprived, but to a lesser degree.

Getting outside help is money well spent, even though it is costly. If you find yourself seriously sleep-deprived and perpetually stressed, find someone to help you, if only for the

> Recognize when you need to ask for help or hire outside assistance.

short term. If I were to do that time over again, I would get help much sooner, probably by the time my son was three months old.

It takes strength and stamina to be a mother. It is a continuing journey, and you need to pace yourself. Eat healthy foods, get sufficient rest, take time to relax and unwind. It's a big challenge to take care of both yourself and your child, so you need to maintain your physical and emotional well-being.

If you are a full-time parent, it's easy to fill every moment with work and caring for your family. But try to take an hour each day to do something you enjoy. This was good advice my mom gave me right after my daughter was born. I didn't realize how wise her suggestion was at the time. Doing this will help you restore your peace of mind and will help you maintain a sense of yourself, which is also important to your well-being.

I found that reading each night before bed was enjoyable and something to look forward to at the end of the day. I joined a book group through our Mothers' Club about the time my son was one year old. This gave me an incentive to read because I knew we would discuss the book. Our book group became my lifeline for the next few years. Going to our monthly meetings was the only thing I did just for myself. Each of the six members had young children, so we agreed to be flexible about requiring members to finish reading the book each month. Most of the time, we did finish, though. We read over a hundred books together and enjoyed meeting for almost ten years.

In addition to daily time for yourself, it's beneficial to have a regular weekly break to get away. You could do this while your husband or partner cares for your child. If you are a single mother, plan your break by booking a weekly babysitter, relying on a friend, or trading off childcare with another mother. A complete change of scene will give a significant boost to your mental and physical well-being, providing you with relief from your daily responsibilities and caretaking. Ideally, you'll be able to calm your mind, restore order to your thoughts, and have time to think and act freely.

Do what makes you feel refreshed: rest, see a friend, go to a movie, pamper yourself. Schedule your getaway at the same time each week, to make planning simple. When you're facing challenges during the week, anticipating your break will keep you going. As mothers, we often neglect ourselves or put our needs last. This is not healthy. Looking back, I could have benefited from regular breaks to refresh and revitalize myself, rather than just the occasional breaks I took.

Meanwhile, continue to nurture friendships you've developed with other parents. Spend time together. Plan social outings with families who have similar-age children. Go out on family "double dates," meeting for early dinners at child-friendly restaurants or sharing simple meals or barbecues at one another's homes. Weekends are great for joint family outings to picnic, go to the zoo or beach, play in the park, ride tricycles and scooters, hike, or even take family trips together. These friendships provide you and your family with support and encouragement. They are important to anchoring you and making you feel connected in your community. This was very true for me and for our family; the friendships and time we shared during these years were very special.

Throughout these years, your child will be active and curious, with no sense of possible danger. She'll want to explore and play, while you keep up with her to make sure she doesn't get hurt. Whether you are a full-time mother at home or a full-time or part-time employed mother, when you are with your child, your primary occupation will be to keep her safe, to play with her, and to encourage her while she is busy reacting to and learning about the world around her.

You'll care for your child's daily needs: feeding, clothing, bathing, potty training, teaching, and providing physical, intellectual, and emotional support. You'll be challenged both emotionally and physically. As your child grows, her routines will change. Some days will be easier than others. There is no map or app for this road. You and your child will navigate a meandering path of new discoveries and destinations. At times, you may feel you are on an aimless journey, but this is your chance to discover and travel with your child, to wander and enjoy yourselves together in ways that suit both of you.

Just as it was a challenge to get out of the house when your baby was little, it can now be difficult to get yourself, your children, their gear, snacks, and perhaps lunch and drinks ready and into the car in order to go somewhere. Sometimes you may feel as though you are herding cats. Stay calm—you'll make it. Tuck in a "back-up" supply of patience with your gear. You never know when you'll need it.

Consider exploring somewhere new each week to learn about your neighborhood and surrounding areas. You'll find interesting places

> Get to know your neighborhood and the surrounding community.
> Check out parks, Exploratoriums, museums, hiking trails, etc. for child-friendly activities, family outings, and weekend getaways.

within your town, and others beyond your immediate neighborhood, for pleasant outings. Depending on your schedule, you can plan these excursions during the week or on the weekend. Your child has passed the big milestones of walking and talking, and she is eager to be moving about and challenged by new interests and activities. Parks where she can explore and play in new environs and places where you can take easy hikes and view nature will be rewarding for both of you. Extend your time outside by bringing a picnic lunch or snacks to enjoy.

I have many memories of good times spent at the parks we found in our county. Dark Park was great for hot days. Its dense trees provided shade, and the shallow stream next to the playground was just the right icy cold temperature to cool our feet. Once we found delicious wild blackberries growing near the edge of the stream that we ate right off the vines. Piper Park was a terrific community park, with challenging jungle gyms, monkey bars, slides, lots of sand for digging, and a huge grassy area to run around in. The swings had extra-long chains that let my children soar high over the park when I pushed them. We held our Mothers' Club Halloween parties there each year. Those parties stand out in my mind as sublime reminders of my young children, caught up in high spirits, playing with friends, while we all enjoyed the lingering embrace of late autumn's warmth and beauty.

Creekside Park was closest to home and was our go-to park. Our favorite was Pixie Park, which required a small fee for membership and responsibility for its upkeep. We'd go there knowing we would see familiar children and families. The park was completely enclosed and could be accessed only by a member's key. This was a relief, since my son had a habit of disappearing at parks. No matter how much I tried to explain to him that I'd like to know *before* he went to play somewhere else or for him to let me know when he was going to the restroom, he wouldn't tell me. I think he figured if he knew where he was, I must know also. I never got used to his quick disappearances. At least, at Pixie Park, I knew he was in the park somewhere, so I didn't have to go into full-blown panic mode when he disappeared.

The park was spread across hilly and flat areas. This mixture of play areas made it ideal for children of various ages. The hill had a steep double slide that was a bit daunting but a favorite for my children. They'd head to the top of the slide, sit down side by side, and pause for a moment to gather the courage to go down. They'd let go and experience a bumpy, fast ride down its rippled surface. At the bottom, they'd jump off and, animated by their bravery, climb the stairs to go down again. The large, flat area had a pretend kitchen in its small playhouse that my children liked to hang out in. There were climbing structures, baby and regular swings, sandy areas for digging, benches and tables for picnics and snacks, and a restroom. We spent so much time there one summer, I began to mingle Pixie Park's toys and our family's toys in my mind. I remember being at home looking for a toy we had played with at Pixie and wondering why I couldn't find it. Those were happy times, spending our days hanging out and playing at the parks.

Look for children's activities at your local library or bookstore. They may have a weekly story hour or sponsor a children's music hour with a singer. These can become enjoyable regular outings. Children love music and singing, as well as the fun of picking out new books. You may want to purchase favorite books to keep in your permanent library. I treasure the stories and beautifully illustrated picture books we saved from our children's early years.

Enroll in an activity or class through your town recreation department to discover more places and activities. Our town's recreation department offered a nature hiking group for tots and parents. Kristen, Paula, and I enrolled ourselves and our children to go on these hikes. Our guide took us on new trails and taught us the names of native trees and wildflowers. We hiked through canyons of tall trees, meadows of grass and wildflowers, on hilly paths and, after the rain, by streams and waterfalls. Our children loved the trails, always on the lookout for animals and other creatures or unexpected finds. They'd crouch down to examine and pick up acorns, flowers, and rocks, and delight in finding fat, slimy banana slugs.

Your explorations and outings will give you further famil-iarity with your community and neighborhood, as well as an added sense of place and belonging. Later, when your child has outgrown the parks and become too busy to go to some of these favorite spots, you'll drive past them and remember the countless hours you spent there, understanding now how won-derful those simple times were. These locations will be physical reminders that connect you to this time and your child's youth.

Children at this age love the familiarity of repetition. You'll play the same games many times. You may not always have the same enthusiasm for playing your child's favorites over and over. You will have days when you feel overcome by boredom, and your mind will scream for relief. Sometimes your days may feel as if they are stretching on interminably without much to differentiate them, or you may feel adrift without compass or direction. It's okay if you don't love every minute of play with your child. When you can, try to slow down mentally and relax physically to take in these times, to experience them as your child does, at full alert.

Play with your child, on the ground, at her level. She sees novelty and fun in everything and is fascinated. She skips, runs, stops, and responds, with her emotions present and close to the surface. This is the rhythm of childhood. Its energetic tempo captivates her and sweeps her into its midst, compelling her to move with its changing beat. Your child is making discoveries all around, she is learning how to manage and control her body while growing physically and socially, and she is learning to engage and respond to others. She is eager to explore her surroundings, no matter the location, and will enthusiastically inspect and scrutinize every new object. She may be involved, with great focus, and yet in the next moment, become indifferent and abandon what was just of immense interest. She may play happily but then fall apart suddenly from frustration. You won't always foresee these turns. She will be caught up in tactile and imaginative play, learning through feeling, touching, and doing. She'll want to master whatever she is doing immediately.

Your child won't be able to master everything the way she wants to, which will be frustrating for her. Depending on her temperament, the time of day, or if she is hungry, tired, or whatever, she may have a meltdown that leads to a tantrum or tears. This is when you want to be calm amid the "storm" of your child's frustrations. If your child is feeling only mildly bothered, you may be able to explain and walk her through

TANTRUMS

In researching children's tantrums, I discovered that children feel scared when they are having a tantrum. They feel frightened by being out of control.

When my son had a tantrum, I learned it was best to pick him up, remove him from what he was doing, and speak to him calmly. I started by holding him so he wasn't able to hit or kick. Once or twice I wasn't able to hold him, so we went to his bedroom, where I could sit in front of the door to keep him from running out while he continued to flail and yell.

Speaking calmly, I would reassure him, "You're okay; you are having a tantrum. Let's get you calm, and you will feel better soon." I would stay with him until his emotions were no longer controlling him and he felt better. Sometimes we would laugh afterward when I'd imitate his tantrums to show him what it looked like. After lots of hugs, we'd talk through how he was able to settle himself and how to avoid a tantrum or handle it better the next time. He'd recover and go off, ready to play something else. Eventually, he did outgrow tantrums.

the necessary steps to help her accomplish what she is trying to do. For example, if the blocks for the castle she is trying to build keep falling, you can sympathize with her about how disappointing it is to see her beautiful castle fall apart. You can then help her to add each block, showing her how they need to be placed so the castle will be balanced and steady. If this doesn't help overcome her frustration, you may need to distract her with another activity or move her away from the annoying problem. You may need to "work it through." I described this method earlier as what we did when we needed to manage frustration that was about to take control of, or had already taken control of, my daughter's emotions. We'd stop whatever we were doing immediately to focus on managing her temper and feelings. My son's frustrations would often lead to tantrums. I read various books and did research to learn how to best help my son manage and avoid tantrums. *See Box: Tantrums.*

At this age, whether your children are being cared for primarily at home by you or another caregiver, it's good to be prepared for long days spent inside. Even though your children will have outings and playdates and activities, there will be many days when the weather or other circumstances make getting outside tough. To keep yourselves busy and entertained, you'll use a combination of games, toys, puzzles, and crafts. Blankets and sheets, chairs and tables can be used to make forts and tents. Cooking, baking, painting, coloring, watching movies, and reading are all engrossing activities to add to the mix. Toy collections make for especially absorbing play because they offer many possibilities. *See Box: Toy Collections.*

You and your child will use all these items to create games and pretend worlds to keep her interested and engaged. Encourage her imagination. Build villages; create long train tracks and paths for cars and trains to go under tables, beds, or chairs; designate locations for trains and cars to stop for passengers or cargo. You could set up a hospital emergency room, doctor's office, or veterinary clinic. Your child can use her bag of medical instruments to diagnose and treat her

TOY COLLECTIONS

Toy collections give your child ways to mix, play, and be imaginative with the combinations. You can build your child's collection by gradually adding or requesting new pieces for your child's favorite toy collection. When you buy toys or when relatives or friends ask what to get your child, consider adding or requesting an additional piece for a collection.

My son loved the Thomas the Tank Engine trains, books, and videos. It was easy to pick up another train or a piece of track, and to let relatives and friends know he liked to collect Thomas the Tank Engine pieces. He ended up with an impressive collection that he loved to play with for hours at a time.

Other good toys to accumulate for collections are building blocks, construction sets, Legos, and accessories for dolls such as American Girl.

dolls' and animals' illnesses and injuries. Consider turning your pantry into a grocery store and letting your child shop. She can use her play cash register to ring up the prices she wants to charge for each item. You could go out to eat in the "restaurant" you set up at your kitchen table or counter. My children loved to make up their own menus, telling me what items to write down. Then they would order from the menu, and we'd cook or bake the food they had ordered. Of course, we'd enjoy eating our creations afterward.

On long days inside, turn rooms in your home into destinations to "visit." Make the family room, or wherever you keep your child's books, a library. Choose books to read; have a story hour; ask your child to tell you a story, or act one out from her favorite book. Make your TV room a movie theater. This was one of our favorites. We'd design tickets, set up chairs for dolls and stuffed animals, make popcorn, and "go to" the movie. Choose a bedroom or two to be hotel rooms. Your child can act as the hotel receptionist, bellboy, or maid, or be the guest who sleeps or hangs out in the room.

Choose a room in which your child doesn't usually play to be a museum. Enter the room carefully and quietly; give your child the "history" of some of the items in the room. Your long hallway can serve as a bowling alley. We set up unbreakable bottles, partially filled with water (with tops securely screwed on) at the end of the hallway. Then we'd take turns rolling a tennis ball or whiffle ball down the hall to see how many bottles we could knock over. Encourage your child to come up with scenarios for other rooms.

Your rooms will get messy with spills or dirt and clutter each day. If your play areas are child-friendly and easy to clean, this will make for less worry. Designate specific bins, baskets, drawers, and shelves for storing various items. Keep old towels and washcloths handy for spills. Build in time for cleanup with your child. You can make cleanup a game by creating rules and ways to score, based on the number of toys each of you puts away. Play "musical toys," where you each race to pick up a certain number of toys before the music stops. Play Mother, May I? to put away "x" toy, or Simon Says to put away "y" toy. Take turns playing Mother or Simon. You and your child will think of many ways to play cleanup.

Read to your child. The time I spent with my child, or both children, snuggled next to me while we read and looked at the pictures together was always special. These moments are magical, when you see your child become absorbed, knowing the illustrations and story have sparked her imagination to bring the characters and their world to life in her mind. She'll become engrossed in the simple tales, sympathize with the emotions of eccentric and odd characters, and be drawn in by absurd and gentle beings. She'll hold her breath as you read a story about a book-friend's difficulties or treacherous circumstances being faced. She'll laugh at silly situations and unexpected antics. You'll delight in seeing what tickles her fancy. Breathe in the sweetness of heartwarming stories, their poignancy, and their affirmation of goodness, fairness, inclusion, happiness, and understanding. These belong to the friendly and uncomplicated world of early childhood in which your child is living. Hold on to your child's favorite books, and yours too, for your family library.

Keep souvenirs of these times and some of the treasures your child comes across. Make mental notes. Your days and hours may seem to inch by, but in retrospect, you will feel as though they flew by. You will want to remember these times and places. I love the memories of this time in my children's childhood. I can see my son's happy face as I pushed him in a swing at the park, his sturdy trot around the playground; the happiness in my daughter's eyes when she woke up and saw me in the morning; I hear both my children's laughter and repeated cries of "Again! Again!" when we played airplane— flying them atop my feet while I lay on the floor; the devilish look my son had, playing in the tub, when he knew he was splashing me with water; and the satisfied look my daughter had as she pushed her doll in a miniature shopping cart down our garden path while holding on to a bobbing red balloon.

Like the seasons, your days and lives will change. The routines and schedules you follow will change. The phases your child goes through, that seem like they will go on forever, will change as well. Have patience and keep your heart open. Each season has its share of complications and blessings. Your recollections of these times, however, will soon be part of the sweet memories that remain with you and warm your heart forever.

TIPS AND SUGGESTIONS—AGES TWO AND THREE
+ New Tip or Suggestion
∗ Prior Tip or Suggestion to Continue

YOUR CHILD'S WELL-BEING	+ Limit screen time for your child: commonsensemedia.org is an excellent resource for determining limits at every age. + Suggestions for your child learning to help: Begin to help with putting away books and toys. ∗ Continue with playgroup. ∗ Continue reading to your child; show her the pictures. ∗ Put aside your phone and electronics when feeding your child and during one-on-one time. ∗ Talk to your child.
YOUR WELL-BEING	∗ Realize you won't have direct control over your time and energy when you are with your child. Decide what your priorities are for the time you have; be reasonable with your expectations. ∗ Set aside time each day, even if it is brief, to give yourself a break. Establish a meaningful ritual for this time. ∗ Arrange with your spouse, partner, or caregiver to care for your child at a regular time each week to give you time for personal restoration. Do something you enjoy (no tasks). ∗ Be patient with yourself.
FAMILY	+ Eat dinner together as a family. ∗ Explore your local community to find organizations, businesses, and parks that are geared to mother, child, and family-friendly activities. ∗ Find child-friendly restaurants. ∗ Continue using reliable babysitters.
YOUR VILLAGE/ COMMUNITY	∗ Socialize with your neighbors. Plan playdates with neighborhood children.

(continued on next page) ▶

▶ *(continued from previous page)*

YOUR VILLAGE/ COMMUNITY	✶ Consider volunteering within a community organization. ✶ Continue with your playgroup.
ACTIVITIES	✚ Learn about children's activities offered through your town's recreation department and local individuals. ✚ Enroll your child with a friend to participate together.
PRESCHOOL	✶ Be sure your child is registered for preschool. You can continue to research preschools, but it's good to have reserved a place for your child in the meantime. If your child is wait-listed at a preschool(s), check with the school(s) to find out if it's reasonable to expect your child to have a place when she has reached the eligible age.

REFERENCE INFORMATION—AGES TWO AND THREE
☆ SAVE LONG-TERM

☆ **BABY'S IMMUNIZATION RECORDS**
Keep track of your baby's immunizations.
Go to: www.cdc.gov/vaccines/parents/downloads/mile stones-tracker.pdf for a printable immunization schedule.

☆ **BABY'S HEALTH RECORDS—NOTES**
Keep the notes you take at pediatrician and other health-care appointments.

☆ **IMPORTANT CONTACTS REFERENCE LIST**
Create a contact list to post in your home for babysitters and other caregivers: include doctors, caregivers, hospital, emergency phone numbers, relatives, neighbors.

☆ **COMMUNITY GROUP(S)' MEMBERSHIP DIRECTORY(S)**
(if any)

In Chapter Five:

PRESCHOOL

(your child will be referred to as "he")

- Beginning preschool
- New environment, people, activities, and routines for your child
- Access to experienced teachers and resources
- Your child and handling transitions
- Child's artwork and crafts
- Jobs for your child
- Child exploring to organize and make sense of his world
- Child very active physically
- Childhood essence
- Preparedness for kindergarten
- TIPS AND SUGGESTIONS
- REFERENCE INFORMATION

Chapter Five

AGES THREE TO FIVE— PRESCHOOL YEARS

Preschool begins! Your child has fun. The preschool teachers have fun. Parents have fun. Preschool is all about fun, within an engaging and comfortable environment. Your child will be drawn in by the rich play settings, toys and materials, and an array of structured and unstructured activities under the guidance and encouragement of teachers. They will encourage your child's imagination, curiosity, and play with other children. He'll participate in groups, follow instructions, and learn how to move from one activity to another. His world will expand immediately.

He will enjoy new surroundings, new playmates, new toys, new games, and new ways to play. He'll have new routines and new things to think about. He'll begin to be aware of his own likes and dislikes, leading to awareness that other people have feelings and thoughts different from his own. This is a first step to being social.

Regardless of your work or at-home status, you will have a new schedule to adapt to, a new organization and environment to learn about, and new families to meet. Your world will also expand overnight. If you have been an at-home mother, this may be your first opportunity to have some time to yourself, or to focus more on your younger child or children. For me, I was glad to have a break from caring for my two young children at the same time. I was able to have one-on-one time with my son while my daughter was at preschool.

Your child will experience preschool as a wonder of activities. There is art to create by gluing, pasting, painting, coloring, mixing, and shaping. There is music and singing, sand and water play, building, running, climbing, and new friends his own age. There is story time and circle time, learning to take turns, listening and playing games—all under the careful guidance of experienced teachers. It's a time of new beginnings and accelerated growth for your child and his classmates. You will see him blossom and grow in the rich surroundings at preschool.

Take advantage of your preschool teachers' wealth of wisdom about preschool-aged children. They'll have the answers to questions about normal childhood behavior. For example: "Is it normal for my child to still use a pacifier?" *Yes*. Or "Is biting normal?" *Yes, but it should be discouraged right away*. Teachers can help you understand and handle your concerns, based on their years of experience. Their advice can ease your mind. Hearing "You are on the right path" or "Your child is just fine" is reassuring. You may want to ask them

> Preschool teachers have a wealth of experience and knowledge.

for information or reference sources to learn more about a particular subject or issue relating to your child. If needed, they can refer you to specialists for speech, behavioral, or occupational therapy.

Many preschools will have parent education meetings or informal parent gatherings to introduce parents to one another and to discuss parenting and child development. I recommend going. You'll get a chance to meet other parents and to find out about issues you may never have considered. Take advantage of the research and information offered by child development experts. The facts may not concern your child but may apply to your next child or to a friend's child. Keeping up with developmental issues and how they might drive your child's behavior as he grows will be helpful for understanding and guiding him.

> Go to parent education meetings and gatherings whenever possible.

Shortly after my daughter began preschool, her school had an introductory meeting. We met other parents and all the teachers. What I remember most was a statement Mrs. Anstey, the head teacher, made. She told us, "Your child will be just fine if you are a good parent eighty percent of the time!" I felt tremendous relief hearing this. *Wow*, I thought, *I can do this*! I don't have to be a straight-A mother. I can enjoy my children, be responsive and engaged, but if I can't be that way every day, it's okay. Some days I can just be a C-level parent. I felt quite confident that I could achieve an 80 percent average. After all, that's a B-. This is excellent wisdom. Knowing you do not need to handle everything perfectly means you can relax and get rid of the anxiety of thinking everything you do has to be perfect. Your child will not turn out "wrong" or have issues when he gets older.

Your child may be anxious about entering the new environment of preschool when it comes time for you to leave him. This may surprise you, as you've probably been thinking how nice it will be for him to go someplace new, to have new playmates and new experiences. However, he might be thinking, *Hmmm, this is a brand-new place. But hold on . . . why is Mom leaving? Help*! He may burst into tears as the unfamiliarity of it all hits him. Don't panic. The nursery school teachers will make sure your child is happy so you are comfortable leaving him there for the next few hours.

My children's preschool had a game called Pop-up to help children who had difficulty saying goodbye to a parent. We played this with my daughter. When it was time for me to leave, my daughter's teacher, Mrs. Beck, would have her crouch near the exit door to hide from me. While I "wondered" where she went, she would suddenly "pop up" to say goodbye. This would "surprise" me and I'd jump back, reacting and exclaiming at how much she had startled me! My daughter thought this was funny and laughed when we went through this routine each day. She would forget to worry that I was leaving and then go into class, happy to participate in games and play with her preschool classmates.

Familiar routines or habits that become rituals are good for helping your child transition smoothly. It is a significant accomplishment when he is

> Routines can help children manage transitions.

able to say goodbye to you easily. Following the same steps for this transition acts as your child's signal that it's time to join his classmates. Having a routine makes him comfortable about the way things work around him.

There will be many times throughout his day when he needs to stop one activity and go to another. Handling transitions can be a matter of temperament and disposition. For example, it's difficult to disengage your child when he is deeply engrossed in an activity. He needs time to break away, as his imagination and energy are fully engaged. An abrupt end can make your child complain while dragging his feet, or even experience a meltdown.

Your child will handle transitions better if you have a routine for them. Take needing to leave somewhere; this is a tough transition that needs to be made all the time. My children were never eager to leave anywhere. They loved playing at the park, playing at a friend's house, going somewhere and being caught up in their activities. It took me a while to realize I needed to prepare them to leave. Thinking that they could stop playing immediately and come with me when I said, "Let's go!" was not realistic. I was used to getting places on time, while they, naturally, had no concept of time.

If I said, "Let's go!" at four o'clock, expecting that we'd leave immediately to drive fifteen minutes in order to get to a meeting at four fifteen, we would invariably be late. I needed to learn to give my children time to wind down and make the transition gradually. I began by alerting my children ten minutes before I wanted to leave. I'd say "ten-minute warning," and then continue with a warning at five minutes, three minutes, and one minute. Other times, I'd try to shorten the time before we needed to leave by being specific about what they could do, saying, "You can go down the slide two more times, and then we will gather our things and go." Our leaving transitions were not always smooth, especially when I forgot to give them a ten-minute warning, and we had just two minutes left. Sometimes you'll have an unraveling situation to deal with, even when you've tried to manage the transition by using a familiar routine. Your child will be uncooperative for some unknown reason; he may be tired, grumpy, hungry, or just out of sorts. Being able to handle transitions smoothly is a continuing challenge and a significant developmental step for children. So experiment with different approaches to find what routines work best for your child. It's nice to have one to rely on so you can avoid the unpleasantness of having to plead, yell, bribe, or—worst case—pick up your child and remove him while he protests loudly. These scenarios are embarrassing, but most mothers have had, or will have, to deal with them at some point. Give yourself points for survival, and for experience.

Preschool will bring a new set of families to widen your community. This is a time of friendly beginnings. You'll enjoy new connections, which come easily through shared experiences. You might learn from his teacher that your child enjoys playing with a particular classmate, whom you could then invite to spend time outside of preschool with both of you. It's best to make your outing a joint playdate with the child's mother, especially while you are getting acquainted.

> Preschool will widen your community.

You'll have other opportunities to meet parents and your child's classmates through participating in the classroom, parent meetings, class picnics, and working on and attending fundraising events.

Many preschools have fundraisers. This was a surprise to me at first, as I figured that tuition covered the school's costs. Money from fundraising is used to maintain, upgrade, or improve the preschool facility and also to keep tuition costs down. You'll find that most schools have fundraising events and campaigns to supplement their regular operating budgets.

Get as involved as you can and get to know the teachers, other parents, and children at the preschool. Any way you can contribute is beneficial. You might volunteer to help with an art project in the class or work with other parents on fundraising. You and your family will enjoy getting to know the other families from the preschool during these years. Some will become part of your circle of friends and supporters.

Your child will create and enthusiastically bring home a lot of artwork during these preschool years. It's fun to see his delight and the pride he has for his inspired masterpieces. They could have been made from all sorts of ordinary objects and recycled items, such as empty egg cartons, spools, paper towel and toilet paper rolls, collections of old games, puzzle pieces, buttons, ribbon, plastic containers, trinkets, and other odds and ends. I have a gift my son gave me, made by covering a small Altoid tin with blue construction paper and gluing small sand-colored shells onto the top. I love this tiny case and have kept it on my dresser for years to store small items. Looking at it, I think of my sweet young boy and the careful attention he devoted to crafting it, and then his presenting it to me as a gift with love and pride.

The amount of new treasures your child brings home can be overwhelming. Most likely, you will not have the space or the

What to do with all that artwork?

inclination to keep them all. It's not practical. You'll need to find a way to edit this growing collection. My daughter would insist that each piece of her artwork be kept. My friend Thana found an excellent way to handle this. She would take a picture of her daughter holding her art, or sometimes she'd record her daughter telling a story about the art. She could then virtually preserve her daughter's creations. Later, she and her daughter could enjoy the pictures and recordings.

You could collect the artwork your child brings home in a large container and go through the pieces at the end of the year, to save a select few. I did this but some years I didn't have time to look through a container over the summer, so the next school year would begin with the prior year's stuffed container. (Some containers, in fact, are still waiting.) You might send artwork to relatives who'd enjoy receiving something from their grandchild, niece or nephew. Another idea would be to create a designated area in your home to rotate items for display. Use this area to display new pieces; store or discard previous items.

Consider having prints or small books made of the pictures you take of your children, relatives, and friends and the excursions and trips you take together. Your child will enjoy looking at these, either with you or on his own. We filled tin lunch pails with photos of our children with their cousins, aunts, uncles, and grandparents. They would carry the pails around the house and on car trips. They liked to dump the pictures out to pore over them, mixing them together regardless of their order, time, or event. Their favorites were the ones they were in, which meant pretty much every photo was a favorite. Looking at them was a great way to remember relatives in between their visits.

"JOBS" FOR YOUR CHILD

Jobs your child could help with: putting toys away, matching socks, sweeping, raking leaves, straightening his bed, bringing clothes to the laundry, putting clothes away, feeding your pet(s) if you have any, and drying unbreakable dishes or pots.

This is a good age for your child to "help" you with some of the household chores. He is eager to do jobs he sees you doing. His "help" will, of course, make the particular task take longer than if you were to do it alone. You'll need to supervise him and show him how to do each job. Think of this time more as playtime than as actual cleaning or straightening time. If you encourage him, he will feel proud and happy to be able to master a task, and to help you. *See Box: "Jobs" for Your Child.*

No matter what your child does at this age, he will do it with his whole heart. His feelings, experiences, thoughts, and imaginings will be expressed in his emotions without hesitation or reserve. He will throw himself into each interaction, becoming caught up in play and imagination. His emotions are always present: joy and happiness, outbursts and meltdowns. They are part of the energetic, earnest young person you completely adore and are trying your best to nurture and raise responsibly. You work to help your child understand and control his emotions, and hope you are making progress.

Many people will tell you, "Enjoy your children while they are young. This time won't last long." What is it they want you to know? What are they telling you about this time? Your child has progressed from needing complete care as a baby, to the constant attention that was necessary in his early years of mobility, to learning to speak and express himself. Now he is busy trying to make sense of his world. He asks many questions and explores enthusiastically, motivated by constant curiosity. He approaches each encounter and experience without assumptions. He responds with appreciation and is easily and happily engrossed in discovery. The world is fascinating to him. Look and you will see the essence of your child's heart and spirit reflected in childhood transparency. These years are remarkable for the beauty found in their simple routines and the happiness you see illuminated by your child's delight in small pleasures. This time doesn't last, but it is unique and wonderful to share with your child. His world is ideal, and you are his heroine.

When your child begins his second year of preschool, a big question to be answered will be, "Is my child ready for kindergarten?"

Kindergarten Readiness

Preschool teachers will know the guidelines for incoming kindergartners at the schools in your community and will be able to help you answer this question. You may decide to look at private schools as well as your local public school. Each school will have guidelines for age and readiness for beginning kindergartners. Most private schools will have an application process that includes an interview with your child and you. Public schools do not go through this process. Contact your local public school district and review their policies online.

KINDERGARTEN ENTRANCE AGE

Education Commission of the States—Fifty State
Comparison—Kindergarten entrance date cutoff
(https://c0arw235.caspio.com/dp/b7f930007026a9ce
fb46435c95df)

The website may have guidelines for determining how ready your child is to begin kindergarten, as well as the skills they recommend for their beginning kindergarten students.

A few states have added a transitional year of kindergarten (TK), offered for children who miss the state's cutoff date for being five by just a few months. These children attend a transitional year of kindergarten followed by a year of traditional kindergarten or, in some states, the option to enter first grade.

Consider at what age you would like your child to begin kindergarten and whether you'd like him to go to public or private school. Public and private schools will not always have the same age requirement for beginning. States have varying dates for when your child should be five to begin public school kindergarten. Many states require students to be five by September 1; other states push that date to December 1. *See Box: Kindergarten Entrance Age.*

The following discussion is for considering when to send your child to traditional kindergarten when transitional kindergarten is not an option. If your child will be five years old at least three months before the school's cutoff date for beginning kindergarten, you may not need to think much about when to start him. If your child has a late summer or early fall birthday, you may want to consider the pros and cons of starting him in kindergarten, since he will be one of the younger children in his class.

Talk with your pediatrician and your child's nursery school teacher. They will be able to guide you, based on their knowledge of your child's maturity and how well he will assimilate into the school. Your preschool teacher can make you aware of an issue you might not have considered, such as your child's small motor skills. If your child's skills are slow in developing, he may have trouble using scissors or a pencil. This could slow him down and be frustrating for him in kindergarten.

Visit the school where you plan to send your child. Ask for a class visit. You'll be able to see the kind of activities and academic learning in which the children are participating. Keep in mind, you will want to consider your observations based on the time of year you are visiting the class. The children will not be as advanced in the fall as they will be later in the school year.

Many parents of boys begin their son in public kindergarten when he is five or older. The idea that boys mature slower than girls is a large factor in this decision. Another consideration is that the extra time allows their son to grow, giving him a better chance to play sports competitively during his school years. The same decision regarding sports can certainly be true for girls as well.

It may seem easy to decide on waiting to send your boy until he is five; the same may not be true for determining when to send your girl. Put aside the notion that "girls mature faster than boys," and consider also where your girl's age places her in comparison to the other girls' ages in her grade. She can certainly be intellectually capable of the work required for each grade level. However, if she is one of the younger girls in her grade, it is important to think beyond this and consider her social maturity. Keeping up with children who might be almost a year older may create challenges or other difficulties for her as a younger child in her grade.

If you have friends or relatives with children who have already gone to kindergarten, ask for their opinion and experience regarding what age is best to send a child to kindergarten. After you've gathered information, opinions, and advice, you can discuss them with your spouse or partner. You'll make the best decision by combining your information, discussions, knowledge of your child, and instincts.

Once you have decided when and where your child will go to kindergarten, take him there to show him where he will be going to school. You can begin to talk about what he will be doing there. Find books to read with him about what he can expect on his first day and beyond.

Many schools have informal gatherings or an orientation for parents of incoming kindergartners shortly before school begins. It may be given by the Parent Teacher Association (PTA) or by the school's administration. Inquire about this when you enroll your child. Attending an event like this will help ease your jitters. If you meet parents who have a second or third child beginning kindergarten, be sure to ask them for advice. They may have helpful knowledge to pass on to you.

Meanwhile, enjoy your preschooler's high spirits and his wholehearted embrace of the world around him. You'll be enriched by the connections you make in your preschool community and touched by the magic your child finds in these years. These are times to treasure and preserve in your memory as a layer of your family history—deliciously dense and forever sweet.

TIPS AND SUGGESTIONS—PRESCHOOL	
+ New Tip or Suggestion ✱ Prior Tip or Suggestion to Continue	
CHILD'S WELL-BEING	+ Arrange playdates with your child's preschool classmates. + Continue reading to your child; show him the pictures and begin to show him the letters and words as he gets closer to kindergarten, if he is interested. ✱ Limit screen time for your child: common sensemedia.org is an excellent resource for determining limits at every age. ✱ Suggestions for your child learning to help: Help with putting away books and toys. ✱ Continue with playgroup. ✱ Put aside your phone and electronics when feeding your child and during one-on-one time. ✱ Talk to your child.
YOUR WELL-BEING	✱ Realize you won't have direct control over your time and energy when you are with your child. Decide what your priorities are for the time you have; be reasonable with your expectations. ✱ Set aside time each day, even if it is brief, to give yourself a break. Establish a meaningful ritual for this time.

(continued on next page) ▶

▶ *(continued from previous page)*

YOUR WELL-BEING	✳ Arrange with your spouse, partner, or caregiver to care for your child at a regular time each week to give you time for personal restoration. Do something you enjoy (no tasks). ✳ Be patient with yourself.
FAMILY	✳ Eat dinner together as a family. ✳ Explore your local community to find organizations, businesses, and parks that are geared to mother, child, and family-friendly activities. ✳ Find child-friendly restaurants. ✳ Continue using reliable babysitters.
YOUR VILLAGE/ COMMUNITY	✚ Go to parent education and parent meetings. ✚ Get to know parents and children at your child's school. ✚ Volunteer at school if possible. ✳ Socialize with your neighbors. Plan playdates with neighborhood children. ✳ Consider volunteering within a community organization. ✳ Continue with your playgroup.
ACTIVITIES	✳ Learn about children's activities offered through your town's recreation department and local individuals. ✳ Enroll your child with a friend to participate together.
PRESCHOOL	✚ Get to know your child's teacher(s) and the school directors. ✚ Take advantage of their knowledge of preschool children's development. ✚ Get answers to questions you may have.
PREPARING FOR KINDER-GARTEN	✚ In your child's second year of preschool, explore kindergarten options and your child's readiness for kindergarten. ✚ Visit the kindergarten campus with your child before kindergarten begins.

REFERENCE INFORMATION—PRESCHOOL
☆ SAVE LONG-TERM
⇨ ENTER INFORMATION IN PERSONAL CALENDAR
❖ SAVE FOR THE CURRENT PERIOD

☆ CHILD'S IMMUNIZATION RECORDS
Keep track of your child's immunizations.
Go to: www.cdc.gov/vaccines/parents/downloads/milest
ones-tracker.pdf for a printable immunization schedule.

☆ CHILD'S HEALTH RECORDS—NOTES
Keep the notes you take at pediatrician and other
health-care appointments.

☆ IMPORTANT CONTACTS REFERENCE LIST
Keep your contact list updated and posted in your home for
babysitters and other caregivers: include doctors, caregivers,
hospital, emergency phone numbers, relatives, neighbors.

☆ MEMBERSHIP DIRECTORY FOR YOUR COMMUNITY GROUP(S)
(if any)

PRESCHOOL
❖ PRESCHOOL CONTACT INFO AND WEB ACCESS INFO—
if applicable

⇨ SCHOOL CALENDAR
- Enter important dates into your calendar.

☆ PRESCHOOL CLASS ROSTER
- Children's and parents' names
- Addresses
- Phone numbers, e-mail addresses

(continued on next page) ▶

▶ *(continued from previous page)*

⇨ **SCHOOL CALENDAR FOR NEXT YEAR:** Obtain when available for planning purposes; enter all dates in your personal calendar.

ACTIVITIES

❖ **ACTIVITY(S) CONTACT INFO AND WEBSITE(S) ACCESS INFO**—if applicable

⇨ **ACTIVITY SCHEDULE:** Enter all dates in your personal calendar.

⇨ **CAR POOL SCHEDULE(S)** (if any): Enter all dates in your personal calendar

☆ **ACTIVITY ROSTER(S)**

- Children's and parents' names
- Addresses
- Phone numbers, e-mail addresses

In Chapter Six:

KINDERGARTEN

(your child will be referred to as "she")

- Age range: four to six
- Beginning kindergarten
- Reflections on starting kindergarten
- Back-to-school
- School and teacher communication
- Join the PTA
- "It takes a village"—importance of community
- School volunteer opportunities
- Kindergarten learning
- Review kindergartener's take-home items
- "Grow" healthy children
- TIPS AND SUGGESTIONS
- REFERENCE INFORMATION

Chapter Six

AGE RANGE: FOUR TO SIX—
KINDERGARTEN

Kindergarten! Sending your child off to kindergarten is a huge milestone! It will be a big adjustment for you and your child. This is the beginning of what may seem to be an unending stretch of years when your lives revolve around school days and school calendars. (Considerations for when to send your child to kindergarten are discussed in *Chapter Five*.)

The first day of kindergarten! The air will feel crisp and fall-like, or maybe it will still be hot and humid. Regardless of the weather, you'll have a sense of excitement and maybe a small knot in your stomach. Amid the excitement, take a picture of your child before she heads off for her first day, to document the first of her thirteen first days, from kindergarten through her senior year of high school. Perhaps you can get to school a bit early that day; go to the playground or the outside area where the children gather before class. Whether you think your child may be anxious or not, she may enjoy seeing the other children as they arrive with their parents and gain confidence from doing so.

The bell will ring, and it will be time for your child to go in to class. The best scenario would be that you say goodbye to her as she happily enters the classroom without looking back at you. This will let you know she's ready to discover this new world of kindergarten.

If your child is anxious, know that her teacher will be ready to handle her nervousness and welcome her into the class and activities. At the end of the day, talk with the teacher to see if your child was able to handle her day smoothly. If not, ask the teacher what she suggests to make it an easier adjustment. She may agree to let you come into the classroom early with your child each day or sit outside at the playground during recess or lunch time. After doing this for a short period, going forward, if your schedule allows, you could volunteer for activities in her classroom from time to time, giving your child reassurance and confidence through your presence.

As you leave your child, other parents will be leaving their children at kindergarten for the first time too. You will all be caught up in the emotion and excitement of this day. You may not think of this at present, but some of these children will share the next thirteen school years with your child as you will share these years with many of their parents.

I remember quite clearly leaving my daughter at kindergarten. She didn't look back! The teacher closed the door, and I walked away, feeling dazed. I thought, *Now what?* I had focused so much attention on getting her ready for kindergarten that I hadn't thought about how I would feel when I actually left her there. Now I was literally shut off from my child. Two years later, when my son went to kindergarten, he didn't look back either. Of course, being a second child, he had been around the school campus for two years and felt like he already belonged. He also knew many incoming kindergarteners, as he had met them on the playground after school each day when he and I, and other parents, came to pick up our children after school.

As I left my daughter at kindergarten that day, my son, who was three and about to begin preschool, was with me. Together we went off to take a walk and to get something to drink. I got hot chocolate for my son and coffee for myself and tried to sort out the confusing thoughts and feelings I was experiencing. I felt like I was in a bit of a daze. My daughter had grown enough to begin kindergarten! *Wow!* and *Huh?* were my most prominent thoughts, not very illuminating or descriptive. But I knew this was the beginning of a new phase for my daughter, for me, for my son, and for our family. I didn't have much time to think about what this meant as I was still taking care of my son. But it did mean I would now have extended alone time with him for the first time in his three and a half years.

When it was time to pick up my daughter after school that first day, my son and I went to the kindergarten playground. We wanted to be right there when the bell rang and my daughter emerged from her first day of kindergarten. Other parents were waiting too. We greeted each other and asked one another, "Do you have a boy or a girl?" "How did your child do, going in to class?" "How did *you* do with your child starting kindergarten today?"

Our common experience gave us an immediate connection with one another. The gnawing hole in my stomach and the hyper level of alertness that had been with me all day began to recede as we talked about our children, their new beginnings, and how these events were affecting us. I realized we all felt much the same way. What was common for each of us was the pride we had in our children and excitement for these new beginnings. This was mixed with our apprehension of the unknown, not knowing how our children were doing, and hoping they would be fine.

Our children were animated as they burst out of the classroom at the end of that first day. They were happy to see us and ready for snacks and some downtime.

Going forward, each day after school, an assortment of parents and caregivers would be waiting for our kindergartners. We'd meet and talk. Those of us with younger children could let them play on the playground while we waited. It was pleasant and easy to spend time together this way. Gradually, we began friendships and became familiar with one another as neighboring families.

If you are a mother who is employed or won't be able to be at pickup each day, you can get to know other families, but you'll do so at different times. If a caregiver picks your child up after school, ask her to look for other children with caregivers. It will be helpful for her to know others she can share information with, or answer questions she may have. If your child is enrolled in aftercare at school, get to know other children in aftercare and their mothers. A good time to meet these mothers will be when you are picking your child up from aftercare. Connecting with them is important. Knowing them will help you build a network of mothers with similar schedules and concerns. Their families, like yours, may need to arrange meetings, playdates, and get-togethers on weekends and other times that require planning around a work schedule.

Back to school brings requests for information, forms to complete, Back-to-School Night and other "back-to" meetings. Most schools' websites have the required forms you need to complete. They will have other administrative information:

Knowing how the school and teachers communicate with parents and send out information is important.

phone numbers, e-mail addresses, the school calendar, news links, parent portal access, and more. You will receive information on how to access the parent portal to retrieve your child's information. Be sure to learn how your school and teachers communicate with parents. Does your school expect parents to check for updated information and announcements, or will they e-mail parents with this information?

When you go to Back-to-School Night, find out how your child's teacher likes to communicate with parents. Does she prefer to do so informally, talking with parents for a minute before or after school, by text, or more formally by phone or voice mail, e-mail, or by scheduling a meeting? Many teachers have their own websites. If your child's teacher has one, she'll let you know how you can access it.

School directories are a "must-have."

Most PTAs and Parent Associations will produce an annual school directory for their members that will include contact information for teachers and administration, the school calendar and bell schedule, as well as PTA and Parent Association information. One of the most important components of the directory is the student section, which includes students' names, grade levels, addresses, phone numbers and/or e-mail addresses, and their parents' names. Address information is especially useful when it comes to ride-sharing, car pools, and playdates. The directory is a "must have" reference item to obtain and hold onto, even after the school year has ended. Being able to go back and refer to it is helpful when you are trying to remember a child's name, who was in your child's class, the name of a teacher, or other information.

When your child begins kindergarten, you'll enter a new community with new ways to expand your connections. When I first became a mother, I hadn't heard the African proverb "It takes a village to raise a child." When I did hear it, I understood its wisdom. By the time my daughter was in kindergarten, our family was part of a village of friends and supporters that had grown in number since we'd become parents. I was fortunate to share the early years of motherhood with a core group of mothers, most of whom I'd met through the Mothers' Club and our neighborhood. Our time together, helping one another manage demanding and sometimes overwhelming times, drew us into a circle of mutual support and friendship. The generosity and pleasure of my friendships with Paula, Kristen, Lesli, Thana, Janet, Judi, Mary, and my sister Margaret meant the world to me in these years. They helped me to be a better parent. I met other supportive parents when I volunteered at my children's preschool and spent time together at our kids' activities.

You'll share the path of parenting with many mothers, fathers, teachers, coaches, school administrators, counselors, and other caregivers. Some will become part of the village you rely on while raising your children. Some will be friends while your children are in the same activity, classroom, or school, but will fade away when your lives no longer intersect. Others will develop into lasting friends with whom you will share memories of your children growing up together.

You'll want to be connected to your child's school community and to parents of your child's classmates, regardless of your status as a stay-at-home mom, or full-time or part-time employment. The easiest way to be involved is to become a member of the PTA. If your child attends a private school, join the school's Parent Association. The PTA functions as a liaison between parents, school administration, and teachers. These monthly meetings will keep you informed of school issues and activities. If you can't attend each meeting, go on your school's website to look for bulletins, a PTA link, or a summary that will keep you up-to-date. Many PTAs and Parent Associations will sponsor speakers and activities, as well as fundraising events. Each of these is a worthwhile occasion to attend, with opportunities to connect with parents and experts. You'll learn about current issues related to your child's age group and other issues affecting your child's school and community.

> Become a member of the PTA.

I knew I wanted to be involved at my daughter's school, so I joined the PTA and volunteered. The first job I took on was hospitality, which I shared with another mom. I found I liked working as a co-volunteer. Collaborating together made the job easier, and working together was a good way to get to know my co-volunteer better. The hospitality position called for us to arrange and present events for parents or teachers. We gave a back-to-school parents' coffee, a holiday lunch for the teachers, and provided refreshments at meetings and other occasions. It wasn't a glamorous job, but I met many parents, teachers, and school administrators in this volunteer role. The annual holiday lunch for the teachers was a large and meaningful event to thank them for doing tough, and often thankless, jobs. This position was the start of many years of volunteering with other parents in my children's schools. You'll see, as I did, that schools always need volunteers. Your work as a volunteer will always contribute to making your child's school better.

If you have limited time for being on campus, try to be there for select occasions, meetings, and volunteer opportunities. As

> Choose volunteer activities based on your time availability.

an example, if your school has a grade-level meeting for parents and teachers, pick that meeting to attend. You'll get an overview of the coming year, from curriculum to social development. If your school needs volunteers to drive for a field trip, do this. Take a personal day or get a caretaker for your younger child or children if needed. You'll be able to spend more time with the children, teachers, and other parents than if you just stopped in for a brief volunteer job.

When you are at school or in the classroom, you'll get a sense of your child's school environment and meet other parents with whom you can talk and share notes, experiences, and possible concerns. You can choose to volunteer in the classroom, in the library, on the playground, or elsewhere. When my daughter was in kindergarten, I volunteered to read to her class in the school library. I liked seeing the children's faces upturned, intent on the story as I read to them, waiting eagerly to find out what would happen next. During my son's kindergarten year, I helped once a week by packing up the children's Friday take-home folders. It was fun to be in class, watch the children immersed in their activities, and see the work they'd done that week as I put each child's work into her folder.

Once your child settles in and feels familiar and comfortable with kindergarten, you will see that she is learning and expanding her horizons rapidly. In public kindergarten, she'll be learning the sounds that letters make, putting letters together for sounds and then into short words. She'll learn the meaning of counting, adding and subtracting, colors, the body's senses, and a bit about science **Kindergarten learning** and nature through a school garden or by observing the life cycle of a butterfly from egg, to caterpillar, chrysalis, and finally butterfly. She'll participate in show-and-tell and will bring home artwork and examples of printing. In private school kindergartens, such as Waldorf or Montessori, children will learn within a less structured environment. These schools focus on socialization and creativity, with children learning at their own pace.

If you come on campus to be with the kindergarteners, you'll be drawn in by their energy. They are a busy hive of happy kinetic energy, buzzing from one task or activity to the next. Even when they are quiet, you can feel their energy flowing as an undercurrent that wants to burst into movement and discovery. Their exuberance is infectious. It's a delight to be in their midst!

At home, take time with your child to look at items she has brought home from school. This habit will reconnect you in the evenings; you'll see what she is working on and hear about her day. She may have artwork, a craft, an announcement from the teacher, a show-and-tell assignment, or the day's schoolwork. Set aside time, also, to read to your child or to listen to her as she reads. She will start with a few simple sounds or words that will increase as the year continues. Your attention will encourage her progress.

At some point while you are raising your children, you may think about the kind of environment in which you'd like to do so. Being a gardener, I thought of raising and nurturing our children in that context. A conversation my husband and I had with our neighbors, Arnold and Sylvia, early in our marriage before we had children, reflects this thinking. They were empty nesters who welcomed us with warmth and hospitality when we moved next door to them. We were outside chatting with Arnold one day when he urged us to "grow some babies." It was an unusual and unexpected suggestion, but I was charmed by it. It might have been an expression from his native country of Latvia, but the analogy made sense to me. As parents, this is what we are doing; we are growing our children in the garden of our home and community. We are tending our children with care, teaching and guiding them within the boundaries we shape to shelter them as they grow.

Like a healthy plant grown in fertile soil, sprinkled by the rain, and warmed by the sun, we all wish our children to be

"Growing" healthy children

blessed with health and an abundance of buds that hold the promise of a blossoming future. We have faith that the seeds, hidden from our view, will form roots and be nourished by our care. We trust that the sun will shine, providing warmth and energy to fuel the emerging sprouts. We hover over them, sheltering the tiny shoots from unfriendly elements, and continue our care. The shoots become thicker, form stems, and develop leaves while gradually buds appear, gather color, and grow in size, ready to open. Unfurled, we bask wholeheartedly in their revelation.

This is a year of transition for you and your child. She is moving from young childhood and informal school into a more structured day and environment. It's bittersweet to see her take this next step, but she will continue to grow, sustained by the security of your love and guidance. Just as sunshine is vital for plants to grow, love is the essential sunshine our children need to grow. Nourish your child to the bone with your love and root her in the comfort and care within your family and home. She will thrive and blossom.

I hope you are thriving too, dear Mom. Immerse yourself in the wonder and curiosity that lives in your Kindergartener; enjoy this year and bloom together.

TIPS AND SUGGESTIONS—KINDERGARTEN + New Tip or Suggestion ∗ Prior Tip or Suggestion to Continue	
YOUR CHILD'S WELL-BEING	+ Spend time with your kindergartener looking at the items she brings home. + Read with your child each day. Show her the letters and words. ∗ Schedule playdates for your child with classmates. ∗ Limit screen time for your child: common sensemedia.org is an excellent resource for determining limits at every age. ∗ Jobs for your child: help put away books and toys. ∗ Put aside your phone and electronics when feeding your child and during one-on-one time.
YOUR WELL-BEING	∗ Realize you won't have direct control over your time and energy when you are with your child. Decide what your priorities are for the time you have; be reasonable with your expectations. ∗ Set aside time each day, even if it is brief, to give yourself a break. Establish a meaningful ritual for this time. ∗ Arrange with your spouse, partner, or caregiver to care for your child at a regular time each week to give you time for personal restoration. Do something you enjoy (no tasks).
FAMILY	+ Family vacation plans will need to coordinate with school breaks. ∗ Eat dinner together as a family. ∗ Get out with your spouse/partner regularly for date night.
YOUR VILLAGE/ COMMUNITY	+ Join the PTA or Parent Association; go to meetings. + Consider volunteering with the PTA/PA. ∗ Get to know parents and children at your child's school.

(continued on next page) ▶

▶ *(continued from previous page)*

YOUR VILLAGE/ COMMUNITY	✱ Stay in touch with your mom friends from playgroup and other organizations. ✱ Volunteer at school if possible. ✱ Socialize with your neighbors. Continue playdates with neighboring families.
ACTIVITIES AND/OR AFTERCARE	✚ Learn about children's after-school activities offered on or off campus through your school, town recreation department, or local individuals, as soon as they are available (usually two months before the quarter begins). Enroll your child with a friend, if you can. Sign up ASAP, as spots fill quickly. ✚ Sign your child up for aftercare, if needed.
KINDERGARTEN	✚ Go to Back-to-School Night to meet your child's teacher. Find out how the teacher communicates with parents, e.g., email, website, voice mail, etc. ✚ Review take-home items with your child. ✚ Learn how school administrators communicate with parents. ✚ Look at school communications routinely to keep up-to-date. ✱ Go to parent education and other parent meetings.
PRIVATE SCHOOL	✚ Research elementary schools if you are considering alternatives to the local public school.
SUMMER CAMPS/ ACTIVITIES	✚ Look at options in January. Sign your child up with a friend (if possible).

REFERENCE INFORMATION—KINDERGARTEN
☆ SAVE LONG-TERM

⇨ ENTER INFORMATION IN PERSONAL CALENDAR

❖ SAVE FOR THE CURRENT PERIOD

☆ **CHILD'S IMMUNIZATION RECORDS**
Keep track of your child's immunizations.
Go to: www.cdc.gov/vaccines/parents/downloads/milest
ones-tracker.pdf for a printable immunization schedule.

☆ **CHILD'S HEALTH RECORDS—NOTES**
Keep the notes you take at pediatrician and other
health-care appointments.

☆ **IMPORTANT CONTACTS REFERENCE LIST**
Keep your contact list updated and posted in your home for
babysitters and other caregivers: include doctors, caregivers,
hospital, emergency phone numbers, relatives, neighbors.

☆ **MEMBERSHIP DIRECTORY FOR YOUR
COMMUNITY GROUP(S)**
(if any)

KINDERGARTEN

❖ **SCHOOL ADMINISTRATION CONTACT INFO AND
WEB ACCESS INFO**

⇨ **SCHOOL CALENDAR:** Enter important dates in your personal
calendar. You may be able to download and sync the school
calendar with your online calendar (if available at your school).

☆ **KINDERGARTEN CLASS ROSTER**
- Children's and parents' names
- Addresses
- Phone numbers, e-mail addresses

(continued on next page) ▶

▶ *(continued from previous page)*

⇨ **SCHOOL CALENDAR FOR NEXT YEAR:** Obtain when available for planning purposes; enter all dates in your personal calendar.

☆ **SCHOOL DIRECTORY**

ACTIVITIES

❖ **ACTIVITY(S) COACH/INSTRUCTOR(S)' NAME AND CONTACT INFO**

❖ **WEBSITE(S) ACCESS INFO—** if applicable

⇨ **ACTIVITY SCHEDULE(S):** Enter all dates in your personal calendar.

⇨ **CAR POOL SCHEDULE(S)** (if any): Enter all dates in your personal calendar.

☆ **ACTIVITY ROSTER(S)**
  - Children's and parents' names
  - Addresses
  - Phone numbers, e-mail addresses

In Chapter Seven:

FAMILY ORGANIZATION

(Your baby/child will be referred to
as "he" or "she" alternatively)

- Responsibilities of motherhood and parenting
- Reflections, discussion, and thoughts on learning how to adapt and manage
- Systems for organizing and managing day-to-day family living and family reference information
- Family Organization

PART 1: CALENDARING

- Calendar
- How to Plan and Schedule Your Family Calendar

PART 2: ORGANIZE YOUR HOME AND IMPLEMENT ROUTINES

- Organizing Your Home
- Create Routines for Common Tasks and Obligations—Suggestions
- Tips for Handling Too Many To-Dos

PART 3: MANAGE INFORMATION

- Know What Information to Save and How to Save It
- Family Reference Information Tables
  1. Family Health Care
  2. Household and Auto—Service and Maintenance Providers
  3. School and Activities
  4. Social, Entertaining, and Vacations

Chapter Seven

FAMILY ORGANIZATION

Your baby has arrived! You and your spouse or partner, or perhaps you alone, welcomed your new baby home. Suddenly, your time no longer belongs to only you, and there seems to be much less of it than before Baby arrived. You are on call 24/7 for your new little one.

You've noticed it takes much more effort to get anything done. You have many new things to learn to do and to keep track of for Baby: feeding, changing, bathing, more laundry, pediatric appointments, and an array of baby care products to keep on hand. Any task or errand takes longer. I remember, just to go out with my infant daughter, trying to get her into the Baby Bjorn took me five attempts to snap it properly while both she and I became increasingly agitated.

As I gradually emerged from the fog of new-baby disorientation, I hoped to find ways to counteract the dazed and off-balance feelings I had. I wanted to be able to handle my new responsibilities with ease, without having to consider each small detail. I found it hard to think through all the steps I needed to take before I could accomplish even simple undertakings.

I am an organizer by nature. I like to be able to plan ahead and take care of jobs or duties routinely and consistently. Being Mom threw me completely out of sync. I felt compelled to find ways to be organized more systematically. Over the years, and throughout my children's many stages of growth, I developed plans and routine ways to complete regular responsibilities efficiently. I organized our home to incorporate these routines. I set up areas to place specific items so I could count on knowing where to find them. I designated a spot in a high-traffic area for items that needed follow-up so I would see them. Each routine, our home organization, and methods of keeping information and schedules up-to-date made our days run smoother. My overall goal was to keep it simple!

In this chapter, I will talk about organization, the routines that helped me, and how I kept up-to-date with our family's schedule. Additionally, I'll discuss the large amount of information families accumulate and how to sort through, manage, and store it so you have it available when you need it.

Over the next eighteen years, you will be immersed in caring, nurturing, and raising your child. This is a lot to think about. Don't worry. It's natural to be overwhelmed at times. Your journey is a marathon, not a sprint; you can only move forward one step at a time. You are beginning as a novice, but you will add to your knowledge and ability every day on this open-ended course. You may feel lost, overwhelmed, or exhausted at times. But you will adapt, learn how to cope, manage, and develop your own shortcuts to become more efficient. Stop when you need to revive yourself, and don't hesitate to turn around or change direction when you get off track. If you are disorganized and bewildered, don't worry, especially as you begin motherhood. Your primary concern is your baby's, as well as your own, well-being. Functioning with little sleep while taking care of your baby is enough to get through at first.

When your world becomes less overwhelming, you can begin to think about better ways to manage. Discuss with your spouse or partner how you can work together to handle each responsibility. The idea is to find a reasonable balance that works for both of you, no matter who is employed full-time, part-time, or is at home with Baby. Realize you're likely to switch, add, or subtract who handles which tasks as time and circumstances change and evolve over the years your child is at home. Experiment with different approaches.

> Discuss with your spouse or partner how you can work together to handle responsibilities. Find a reasonable balance.

Until your child is self-reliant, her needs will require much from you physically. You and your spouse or partner will be handling every one of her needs, from feeding her, cleaning her, and keeping her entertained and safe, to dressing her and attempting to maintain a practical schedule for her. Having a child in your family means you and your spouse or partner will have less time for your own lives and activities. Work, exercise, personal interests, friends, your relationship, and leisure will all be affected. You won't always have the time you would like for each of these.

In many ways, you and your spouse or partner will resemble jugglers working together, tossing responsibilities back and forth and into the air, while attempting to handle immediate issues closest at hand. If you are a single mother, you'll be doing even more juggling, with higher tosses and more items in the air. You'll want to find a reliable helper(s), who can provide you with effective support.

For stay-at-home mothers, unless you have reliable time for yourself, you will see that your ability to do things or go places will depend on your baby's patience. If she is feeling content, has been fed recently, is rested, and does not become overstimulated, she'll be more apt to accompany you happily, to look around with interest, and to light up with adorable baby charm when people notice her. You'll learn to recognize your child's tolerance level. When it's time to head home, you'll know it. It's just not worth doing that one more thing that will likely cause your child to reach the tipping point, melt down in tears, or erupt into a full-blown tantrum.

Your child's temperament is also a factor in your ability to handle responsibilities, aside from caring for him. He may have a temperament unsuited to going out or accompanying you because he is sensitive and easily overstimulated. He may be extremely active and unwilling to stay in a stroller, or if he is too old for a stroller, he may run off, leaving you in a panic.

I am very familiar with how hard it is to go places and run errands when one's child does not want to. My extremely active son never wanted to be in a stroller, ride in a shopping cart, or have his movement restricted in any way. (He had started crawling and walking very early, crawling at five and a half months and walking at seven and a half months.) I had to give up on going to large stores like Costco because I was worried he might run off and be impossible to find. He had done this once at Home Depot when he was about one and a half years old. The entire store was shut down with a "Code Adam" (missing child alert) until we found him in the electronics section.

Another day we were shopping at some stores in our local outdoor mall. I was ready to pay for a purchase at the counter. In the time I took to look into my handbag to get out my wallet, my son disappeared. (He wasn't in his stroller because he had been wriggling and crying so much that I had let him get out for a minute.) Just like that, he took off without a word. I happened to catch a glimpse of him as he was leaving the store. My daughter and I left our items at the cash register and ran out to chase after him. We weren't sure where he went. We searched frantically. With the help of some kind other shoppers, we finally found him two stores away, hiding among a carousel of hanging clothes. I don't know how we even thought to look there.

Occasionally when we had to make unavoidable trips, such as going to our local CVS, it was rough. My son didn't like to be in a shopping cart and would protest by crying loudly when I put him in one, but I had to keep him in the cart so he wouldn't run off. Shoppers would glare at us when he cried. I could see the thought bubbles popping up over their heads saying, "Why do you have your screaming child in the store?" "Don't you know that's annoying?" "Why can't you handle your child?" I knew he was loud and no one wanted to hear his crying, but I wished they could understand I was there only because it was absolutely necessary. It was stressful for me. In general, I tried to take my son on as few errands as possible.

Being stuck at home when you need groceries or some other essential item can make you feel helpless. Find out which of your local stores deliver. Some pharmacies have drive-up windows, which is helpful if you can at least get your child into the car. If you are desperate, call or text a friend to help you out. Don't forget, you would be happy to do the same for a friend if you could, and you'd be glad your friend had called you for help.

Stock up on essential baby and child care items as well as food staples.

Plan for the inevitable times when you won't be able to get out by stocking up on essential baby and child care items as well as food staples. Keep extra diapers, wipes, baby Tylenol, and formula (if needed). When your child is older, keep servings of your child's favorite foods in the freezer. Or prepare and freeze meals in advance. You might do this on the weekends and then freeze the prepared meals. You can double up on cooking some foods to use for a quick prep meal the next day, like extra chicken to use in tomorrow's salad.

Each year, you'll have new things to keep track of. Later, when your child is older and goes to school, her schedule, homework, and activities will increase and overlap, making organization and planning crucial.

It's also smart to set reminders for yourself, particularly if you need to be some place at a specific time. Once, when my daughter was in kindergarten, I forgot to pick her up from her neighborhood art class because I had completely lost track of time. I had been working at her school on a PTA project when I suddenly remembered that I needed to pick her up. I was shocked at how absentminded I had been, especially since I was volunteering at *her* school. I was just a few minutes late getting her, but it made me realize that setting reminders would be a good routine to follow. It's easy to get distracted and be unaware of how much time has passed.

Over time, I began to adhere to a regular approach to scheduling and planning. I became more disciplined about obtaining and maintaining information needed by our family, from activities and school schedules to health and financial records. I worked to simplify regular jobs and responsibilities. I found ways to break these jobs into smaller tasks to do when I had time. I could do smaller portions in advance to cut time needed later, making the jobs more manageable. These habits helped me be more effective and efficient at managing our family's needs. It was a relief to rely on these methods and manage more confidently.

Motherhood is a bustling, bumpy, and busy road. Navigating it can be complicated. I've tried various approaches and have found the road is less daunting when I am organized. Organization hasn't always saved me from wrong turns along the way, but it has given me structure and direction for composing my days and using time optimally in the ongoing quest to keep our family on track.

FAMILY ORGANIZATION

PART 1: CALENDARING

PART 2: ORGANIZE YOUR HOME AND IMPLEMENT ROUTINES

PART 3: MANAGE INFORMATION

There are three parts to the approach I've refined over the years for organizing our family. *See Box: Family Organization.* The rest of this chapter is devoted to explaining each. Use the methods and ideas that make sense to you and that help you manage as you make your own way along the highways and byways of family living.

PART ONE
CALENDARING

SCHEDULE AND PLAN
YOUR FAMILY CALENDAR

The best way to be organized is to stay up-to-date by planning and scheduling your calendar regularly. I call this "calendaring." Putting appointments in your calendar is nothing new, but making time to review your calendar once a week to figure out *how* you will manage all the tasks and needs your family has each week and doing a quick review and update to your calendar at the end of each day will give you a reliable approach to staying on track amid your daily comings and goings.

Calendaring has two parts.

1. First is your actual calendar. Think of it as your map for the week because it gives you the layout of your days and the week. It shows you where you need to be each day and at what time. It contains your appointments, the daily breakdown of your schedule, vacation days, travel days, and more.

WEEKLY CALENDAR

I like a Monday–Sunday weekly calendar. It corresponds with the school and work week. Be sure to include the following in your calendar:

○ Appointments
○ Social dates/playdates
○ Car pool schedules
○ Days off for school (once your child goes to school) and work, vacation, teacher days, and holidays
○ Activities/lessons (include games, meets, and performance dates)
○ Travel dates for you, your child, and spouse/partner
○ Mutual appointments, dates, and travel plans for you and your spouse/partner

☆ KEEP YOUR CALENDAR CURRENT.

- Record appointments in your calendar as soon as they are scheduled.
- Input all dates for ongoing classes, appointments, activities, etc. when you receive those schedules. *See Box: Weekly Calendar.*

2. **The second part of calendaring is compiling *and* organizing your to-dos for the week.** This is the *how* of managing your week. Your weekly to-dos include everything that needs to be done to get you and your family members fed, clothed,

where you all need to be, and when you need to be there. It includes scheduling doctors' and dentists' appointments, social activities, entertainment, taking care of household maintenance, finances, and more.

☆ PLAN YOUR WEEK ON THE SAME DAY EACH WEEK.

Sundays are a good day to get yourself organized for the coming week.

Begin by looking at your calendar to get an overall view of what's coming up. Determine what needs to be done this week. Make your to-do lists.

I have found that dividing my to-dos into separate lists by category makes planning simpler and helps clarify what needs to be done. I use five main categories. *See table: Weekly To-Do List on the next page.*

WEEKLY TO-DO LIST

MISC.

GO   BUY/NEED   DO

CONTACT

DINNER PLANS

Monday

Tuesday

Wednesday

Thursday

Friday

Saturday

Sunday

☆ MAIN CATEGORIES:

MISC. _(Miscellaneous)_

- Fill in notes of things that you want to remember to do _once_ that week arrives, such as reminders, pending items, or miscellaneous notes for the week (Example: Call Liz this week for dinner)

GO   BUY/NEED

- Places you need to go and what you need to purchase or pick up during the week (Example: Go: CVS   Buy/Need: shampoo, Tylenol)
- Grocery Shopping
- Errands/Other

CONTACT

- People to call, e-mail, text, or write
- Arrange appointments, scheduling, playdates, car pools, follow-ups
- Keep in touch with friends, family

_DO_ _(This is usually the largest category)_

- Follow-ups, review, research
- Updates to calendar and scheduling
- Meal planning
- Finance: bill paying, banking, insurance
- Home, yard maintenance
- Other projects

DINNER PLANS

- Plan your dinners for the entire week

- Note your dinner plans: Monday–Sunday. Include how to access recipes: website, cookbook page number, etc.
- Make a grocery list of foods you need for the week: for dinners, breakfasts, lunches, and snacks.
- Shop once a week for most of your groceries. Make a note of any other grocery items you need to pick up later in the week, e.g., "Pick up fresh fish on Thursday for dinner."
- If you want to invite friends over or go out for dinner, plan for these also.

Regular grocery shopping and meal planning, especially dinners, are important elements of managing your week. Once I began to do these routinely, I noticed it helped me immensely. I was able to avoid the late afternoon dread of "What's for dinner?" When you plan your dinners for the week, take into account the amount of time you'll have to prepare dinner by looking at each day's schedule. Choose quickly prepared meals or occasional take-out meals for busy days. You can plan meals that take longer to prepare on days when you have more time. Make a grocery list and do the bulk of your grocery shopping once a week. We usually did ours on Sundays. My husband and I were both at home, so one of us could shop while the other watched our children. During the week, at the end of each day, it was a huge relief to know I had the necessary groceries and ingredients on hand to prepare our meal.

Next, look at your lists and determine:
- **Which items need to be prioritized?** Plan to do these first. Put them in your **DO** section.

EXAMPLE ONE

Add to your to-do list:

○ Contact Robert's mom to get other party guests' names.

○ Arrange a playdate or a ride for Sophie with one of the guests following the party.

Add to your calendar or set as a reminder:

○ Reminder for Thursday or Friday to finalize Saturday plans for Sophie: ride or playdate.

- **Do you or someone need to do something prior to an event?** If so, then record these as new to-dos for the week. Be sure to set or note necessary reminders. *See Box: Example One.* As an example, let's say you have a husband and two children, Teddy and Sophie, who have overlapping activities coming up on Saturday. Sophie's friend Robert has invited her to his birthday party from one to three, and Teddy has a two thirty soccer game. Both you and your husband want to see Teddy's game. This means you need to figure out what to do when Sophie's party ends at three, since neither you nor your husband will be available to pick her up. You could try to find her a ride from the party to the soccer field or arrange a playdate for her with one of the children at the party. To do this, you'll need to contact Robert's mom to find out which other children are going to the party and then follow up with one or more of those children's parents by Thursday or Friday to make your arrangements.

EXAMPLE TWO

Add to your to-do list:
- ○ Schedule time out of office Wednesday, beginning at 1 p.m. (to allow commute time from office to school)
- ○ Reschedule or arrange to handle appointments or obligations at work on Wednesday after 1 p.m.

Add to your calendar:
- ○ Wednesday 1 p.m.: leave office for Sophie's preschool event
- ○ Wednesday 2 p.m.: parent event at preschool

- **Which items may require you to plan in advance?** Then add the to-dos for taking care of these advanced plan items. Again, be sure to add a note to your calendar or set a reminder for each one. *See Box: Example Two.* In this scenario, there is a parent event this coming week on Wednesday at two o'clock at Sophie's preschool. The event is during work hours, which means you'll need to arrange your schedule to be out of the office and reschedule meetings or other items planned for that time.

- **Which days are especially busy; can you prepare ahead of time to simplify those days?** Add these preparatory steps to your to-dos for the week.

☆ DETERMINE A REGULAR TIME EACH DAY TO REVIEW YOUR CALENDAR AND TO-DOS.

(I like to do this at the end of the day so I know what's on board for the next day.)

- Review your calendar to see what is scheduled for the following day.
- Add in any new appointments that you haven't yet calendared.
- Review your to-dos and revise them, as necessary.
- Check off the to-dos you have completed.
- Add in any new to-dos as needed.
- Add in any new reminders as needed.

Together, your calendar and weekly to-do lists show you everything you need to know and do each week. These are the keys to staying on track. You may feel resistant to recording so many details, but it is easy to forget something amid all your responsibilities. When you are certain your calendar is up-to-date, you will be able to rely on it and go about your days confidently.

There are many calendar apps you can download to your smartphone to help you manage your family calendar. The mobile app Family Organizer by Sevenlogics allows you to record and keep track of your to-dos, recipes, and more. (The free version has advertising.) I use the agenda view of WeekCal app for the iPhone.

You may prefer to use a paper calendar so you have a hard copy to keep. With paper calendars, you don't have to worry about battery life or the risk of liquids, food, or dirt destroying the smartphone, computer, or tablet that holds your calendar, although technology is improving to make water and some liquids not as harmful to electronics. Dust and dirt are still dangerous for smartphones, tablets, and computers. If you do use a paper calendar, I recommend a two-page format that has your calendar on the left side and to-do items for the week on the opposite page. You can see your appointments, obligations, dates, and to-do items for each week, without the need to scroll back and forth. For years, I used this method before smartphone calendar apps became more user-friendly. I liked being able to see everything for the week in one place.

I use a smartphone calendar app now but still use a two-page weekly calendar to write out my to-do lists on the blank page opposite to the days of the week. (I like the Moleskine weekly planners.) It organizes my lists in one place and serves as quick reference when needed. (I also like to keep my yearly personal calendars for the memories they hold.)

It's good to always have your calendar with you. Chances are, you will if you carry your smartphone. (If you use a paper calendar and prefer not to carry it, take pictures of your calendar pages for the current week and the next few weeks to store in your smartphone. You can take pictures of lists or notes you have in your paper calendar to have on hand for reference too.)

As I mentioned before, enter new appointments, meetings, playdates, and other events as soon as you schedule them. When you set up a car pool or other obligation that requires you or your child to be someplace or available at a specific time, put this in your calendar immediately. When your child gets older and you receive his activity, team, school, or other schedule, put these dates in your calendar within twenty-four hours. I encourage you to develop this habit to ensure you stay current with each family member's schedule.

I regretted the times I did not put dates in my calendar right away. I remember at the beginning of one baseball season, I picked my son up after school and found out he needed to go straight to the field for a game. I didn't have any of his gear with me because I hadn't looked at his schedule or put it in my calendar yet. This meant I had to drop him off at the field and then come back with his uniform and snack. If I had reviewed his schedule and "calendared" it right away, I could have avoided having to make two trips in busy after-school traffic!

Once you've written down all your to-dos, you may feel overwhelmed, wondering how you're going to get everything done without drowning in desk work, mail, e-mails, and so on. Typically, mothers do more household and child-raising work than fathers. This is where conversations with your spouse or partner about handling the family and household weekly to-dos become meaningful. Discuss these together. The number of jobs and obligations for taking care of your family and home is substantial. It helps to share these responsibilities.

> Divide and conquer tasks and responsibilities with your spouse or partner.

Talk about which items are critical. Determine who is able to handle them, based on time and availability. For example, food shopping and daily meals are a must. Could you split these tasks, with one of you shopping and the other preparing the meals? Or, depending on your schedules, could you split meal preparations, while letting your spouse or partner do cleanup? When your child is of school age, making sure he gets to his homework and to bed on time each night is a daily priority. Paying your bills on time is also a priority. At each stage, decide who can best handle these jobs. Remember, you can always switch or trade off.

If you are a single mother or have a spouse or partner who travels frequently, take care of priority items when your child has a weekly class or an outing. Or schedule a regular time for a babysitter and use that time. If you have an in-home child caregiver, see if she can complete some of these tasks before you return home. For example, she could make dinner and start your child doing her homework.

> Let go of unrealistic expectations for doing everything perfectly.

It may take some time for you to realize and to accept that not everything will get done, or won't always be done on time, or to your liking. (It certainly took me a while to come to this understanding as I mentioned in an earlier chapter.) These are parts of letting go of the unrealistic expectations of managing everything perfectly. It's okay. Do the best you can. Focus on taking care of the essentials: food, rest, health, and paying the bills. You will find suggestions and routines to cope with being overwhelmed next, in PART TWO.

PART TWO

ORGANIZE YOUR HOME AND IMPLEMENT ROUTINES

ORGANIZE YOUR HOME

This section has suggestions for handling the daily flurry and commotion of family life. The idea is to organize your home and implement routines to make everyday tasks and activities simpler. This will help your day-to-day family life run smoothly, or at least as smoothly as family life *can* be. You'll also find ideas to help you get things done when you are feeling overwhelmed. As you know, feeling overwhelmed can come on quickly, often right when you think everything is going well.

The arrival of your baby brings all kinds of new items and products. When your child is an infant, you have the baby care products, which accumulate all over your home until you decide where to keep them. During this phase, you can't worry too much about order and neatness. You're lucky if you're getting enough sleep. One routine I did begin, after my daughter was a month or two old, was to pack up her diaper bag in the evening so it was ready for the next day. I'd place it right by the front door so I could find it when we were finally able to leave. I did this because, while it was a triumph to get my daughter fed, changed, and ready to go out, if her diaper bag wasn't ready, I'd have to spend more time looking for everything that needed to be packed into it and have less time out to accomplish what I needed to get done.

As your baby grows, you'll find that toys, games, and books spread themselves throughout your house and need to be rounded up each day. You'll need ways to corral them quickly. You won't have the time or inclination to place each item neatly back onto a shelf or inside a closet. The easiest way is to group like items in large, open bins, baskets, canvas totes, or drawers. Use bookshelves for more than just books; use them to house bins and baskets of toys, blocks, art supplies, and the like. Once a day, put everything away. By the time your child is two, she will be able to participate in cleanup time. If she wants to help sooner, that's great. Always encourage help.

A Place for Everything and Everything in its Place

Gradually, as you accumulate more stuff and your family has more items coming in that need attention, you'll find it helpful to organize your home by creating an assigned location for each of these. "A place for everything and everything in its place" is a good motto to follow. This way, you can put things away quickly because you know where they belong, and you can save time because you know where to find them. You'll be able to see at a glance if something needs attention or is missing.

It makes sense to designate spots for items that you use regularly or that require timely follow-up. *See Box: Designate Locations in Your Home for Regularly Used Items.* You'll notice

DESIGNATE LOCATIONS IN YOUR HOME
FOR REGULARLY USED ITEMS

Main Exit Door—Ready-to-Go Location

○ Packed diaper bag

○ Stroller

○ Umbrella

○ Car and house keys

○ Sunglasses

○ Backpacks

○ Activities gear needed
  for the day, packed
  and ready

Central Location—Kitchen or Front Hall

○ **Household Inbox**
Use the household inbox for your home maintenance,
finance, medical, insurance bills, correspondence, etc.

○ **Family Inbox**
Use the family inbox for your children's school, activity,
and personal notices, invitations, etc.

○ **Incoming Mail**
Gather and sort mail here; it's okay if it accumulates
for a few days, but be sure to glance through it for any
urgent items.

- Gather follow-up business mail such as bills,
  statements, doctor and medical correspondence,
  other ⇨ Place in your Household Inbox.
- Throw out junk mail.
- Stack magazines ⇨ Place in a reading pile.
- Stack catalogs you want to keep ⇨ Place in a
  reading pile.

○ **Charging station**
Recharge all electronics overnight.

(continued on next page) ▶

▶ *(continued from previous page)*

Family Room, Playroom, Bedroom
○ **Toys, Games, and Books**
Use shelves, bins, baskets, and boxes. Store these, grouped by category in designated spots, near play and reading areas.

Home Office—Filing Center
○ **Household Files, Notebooks, etc.**
Keep these physical files and notebooks together.

---

this list includes a Family Inbox, a Household Inbox, and a Ready-to-Go Location. See explanations in the box for each.

No matter your child's age, there will be regular requests and information from school, activities, organizations, and more that you will need to review and follow up on. It's good to check for these notices daily. Your child will bring home notes from school and activities. Other notices will come in via e-mail or be posted on a school or activity website. Some may have a brief turnaround time, so you will want to have a reliable follow-up system to ensure these items are taken care of promptly. You'll get requests for volunteering your time, donating specific items, driving, and more. When you sign up or commit to these, be sure to record them in your calendar and as an item to do.

Some notices that come in will take time to think through or to vet before you are able to make a decision on how to handle them. In this case, you can print the item out or write yourself a note to place in your Family Inbox for follow-up. Put a reminder in your calendar too. Place your Family Inbox in a high-traffic location where you will see it and remember to take care of the items you have in it. I put ours on the front hall table because I had to pass by it on my way to bed. I made it a habit to take care of the items before bedtime and place them in my children's backpacks or bags so they were ready to go with them the next day.

As much as you try to organize and sift through all of your family's "stuff," you'll most likely have a multitude of items that accumulate throughout the year. It's not always easy to decide on what to keep or save. We found that in the meantime, it was easiest to collect the unsettled things to go through later when we had the time to be more discerning. We accumulated artwork, invitations, birthday cards, souvenirs, sports and extracurricular clothing, equipment, and more. We put everything into a large bin in our children's rooms to go through at the end of the calendar or school year. We would throw out a lot and try to limit to just one box the items that we decided were worthy of keeping. We sent outgrown clothes, toys, and books to younger cousins, gave them to friends with younger children, or donated them. If you have clothes or toys that you want to save for younger siblings to use in the future, store them in bins labeled with the appropriate age. Be sure to keep special and well-loved books, toys, and clothing when you sort through your child's items.

> Once a year, go through your child's toys, clothes, books, artwork, and equipment. Give away items he no longer needs. Save special and well-loved books, toys, and clothes.

☆ IMPLEMENT ROUTINES

In addition to your calendar scheduling, weekly to-dos, family information (covered in Part Three), and home organization, your family needs food, clean clothes, and linens, and your home needs upkeep and maintenance. Over the years, I developed routines for handling many of these repetitive household tasks. These routines include ways for getting food on the table, getting endless laundry done, keeping the kitchen clean, and more. They helped make many of the boring jobs simpler and got me through the humdrum tasks. You'll find these methods in the suggestion boxes shown throughout this section. Try them to see what works for you. Create your own routines for common tasks and obligations..

Being a mother usually means you are perpetually in motion, running around, trying to do five things at once. Having routines allows you to be on "autopilot." This frees your brain to focus on the three or four other tasks that require you to think decisively.

Routines can be used by both you and your spouse or partner. As I mentioned earlier in the chapter, it's important to work together. You may have a naturally helpful spouse or partner and not need to discuss how to keep up your home, care for your child, manage her activities and homework, and look after the rest of the household. Or you may have a spouse or partner who travels frequently or works extra-long hours, resulting in little time for him or her to help. Do the best you can to divide tasks, according to your household situation.

You may each do things differently. This is fine. The important thing is to get the job done, with both of you contributing to running your home. So, if you like your clean towels folded in thirds and your spouse folds them in halves, don't let this bother you; at least the towels are clean and folded.

MANAGING LAUNDRY

○ Always have plenty of laundry soap and other laundry products you use on hand.

○ Do a load of laundry every day. This will keep you reasonably on top of this endless job. Find a time of day that works for you to do washing, drying, and folding.

○ Finish drying clothes when you (or someone) are able to fold them right away. This way your clothes will not sit developing wrinkles, which would mean added time for "touch-up" drying or ironing (the worst!), or having clean but wrinkled clothes.

○ Empty the dryer lint trap after each load. Do this when you take the clothes out. Knowing the lint trap is clean saves you the annoyance of checking. (This is a small suggestion, but it helps.)

○ Know that socks like to hide in the corner pockets of fitted sheets.

Below are suggestions and routines that I've implemented to manage the common tasks and obligations in our home.

Laundry

There is no way to get around laundry. With children, you will have a lot of it. When your child is a baby, you're likely to enjoy seeing her cute little baby clothes and will not mind washing and folding her adorable outfits. Sadly, as your child gets older, her dirty clothes don't seem as appealing, and you are left with piles of boring laundry. See Box: *Managing Laundry*.

Kitchen

When you are at home, you will feel as if you spend the majority of your time in the kitchen. And it will always seem to need cleaning. As a mother, your normal mode of awareness can easily be attention-and-sleep-deprived. This can mean that you might absentmindedly overlook the steps you'd normally take to keep your food preparation area clean. Following routines to keep your kitchen clean can reassure you that you are preparing and serving your family healthy food. *See Box: Keeping the Kitchen Clean.*

Meal Planning and Preparation

It's a big job to feed your family three times every day. This means you need to be prepared with enough food in the house. Natural, wholesome foods are the best nourishment and are so important because you are setting the foundation for your child's future food choices and habits.

When your children are young, the meals you prepare will be simple. My children loved macaroni and cheese, scrambled eggs, chicken, and pasta. Chances are your children will have favorites that they are happy to eat. I know it can get boring making the same things all the time. Ask your friends for recipes their children like. Don't be surprised when your child no longer wants to eat his favorite. This will seem arbitrary, and you won't know what caused your child's taste to change. You may try to persuade him to reverse his decision and be surprised at his refusal. My son did this at one point—abruptly deciding he no longer liked his favorite chicken dish when it was already cooked and on his plate. I couldn't change his mind and decided it wasn't worth trying to overcome his reasoning.

KEEPING THE KITCHEN CLEAN

○ Use a mild scrub sponge for washing dishes.

○ Use a steel wool pad for tough pots.

○ Use a kitchen washcloth for wiping counters.

○ Use one towel for drying the clean dishes.

○ Use a separate towel for drying your hands.

○ Begin each day with a clean kitchen washcloth.

○ Begin each day with a clean towel for drying dishes.

○ Rotate the dish-drying towel to become your hand-drying towel.

○ Use separate cutting boards for veggies and fruits, and for raw meats, poultry, and fish.

○ Use empty waxed paper bags from cereal boxes to protect the kitchen counter from food contamination. You can put them under your cutting board when you are preparing raw chicken or other meats; wrap up leftover raw scraps in them and throw them out right away.

○ Keep paper towels and cleaning cloths or rags close at hand to clean spills on the floor. Never use your kitchen washcloths or towels on the floor. Sweep the floor every day or at least use the quick whisk broom for crumbs.

○ Try to have your kitchen clean, with dishes washed and put away before bed each night. A dirty, messy kitchen is tough to face in the morning

Preparing dinner every night (or almost every night) is tough. Getting stuck at five o'clock with no idea of what's for dinner can make your stomach sink. You'll find suggestions for preparing dinner, avoiding being stuck, and countering the tedium of preparing dinner regularly in the box: *Meal Planning and Preparation.*

MEAL PLANNING AND PREPARATION

○ Use natural, unprocessed foods as much as possible, particularly fruits, vegetables, meats, and fish.

○ Look for and collect fast and easily prepared recipes with short lists of ingredients.

- Look online, in magazines, and in cookbooks.
- Find recipes by joining a recipe provider online like Real Simple Food Recipes.

○ Save your recipes so you can access them quickly.

- Print out or make copies of recipes. I like to have a hard copy of recipes to use while I'm cooking, so I have many recipes saved this way. I put the recipes in clear page protectors to keep them clean and then file them by category in a three-ring binder. Each week I go through the binder, pull out the recipes I plan to use, make my shopping list, and then keep the pages out to use when I make the recipe.
- Use Pinterest boards or the Paprika app to store recipes by category: salad, meat, fish, chicken, etc.
- Put tabs in your cookbooks for favorite recipes, or you could use the Eat Your Books app that will index recipes from cookbooks you own and magazines or blogs you read.

(continued on next page) ▶

▶ *(continued from previous page)*

- Plan your dinners to coincide with your weekly schedule, using quickly prepared recipes or take-out food to pick up on busier nights.
- Make lists of favorite recipe ingredients and store the lists in your smartphone. You'll be prepared with a list of what to buy if you're out and need to pick up ingredients for dinner.
- Try to shop for the bulk of your groceries once a week. You can make a quick stop later in the week for additional fresh vegetables or meats.
- You may want to subscribe to a meal service for one or two dinners each week, to have recipes and ingredients delivered straight to your home.
- Begin dinner preparation before evening. You or your spouse or partner could do some prep in the morning before you leave for work or, if you are home during the day, when you are in the kitchen with a couple of minutes to spare.
  - Get out your dinner preparation items: pots, pans, stirring spoons, spatulas, knives, measuring utensils, and any dry and nonrefrigerated ingredients.
  - Set out dinner plates, flatware, and glasses. You can do this easily in three or four minutes. (It's a good task for young children to help with and that they will enjoy. Older children can help too, even if they don't enjoy it as much.)
  - These simple steps done ahead of time will make preparing dinner less overwhelming and speed you through the "witching hour" that occurs when everyone first gets home and is hungry and tired. You'll be able to make dinner quickly because you'll already have most of the items you need out and ready to go.

Handling Too Many To-Dos

It's tough to get anything done when you are overwhelmed. If you are truly exhausted and your to-dos are not critically important, you will be better off resting and trying to tackle the jobs, obligations, or responsibilities later. Otherwise, try one or more of the suggestions in the box *Getting Started on Too Many Things to Do*. These work for me because they get me *started*. Usually, once I *begin to work* on something, I feel motivated to keep going and forget how much I didn't want to do "x" task. Often, I will then continue on to do "y" task and even "z" task.

Bill Paying

Bill paying and budgeting are two more big jobs. They are discussed further in *Chapter Eight, Family Finances and Safeguards*.

GETTING STARTED ON
TOO MANY THINGS TO DO

○ Set a timer for ten minutes to see how much you can get done within that time. This works for quick kitchen cleanups or emptying the dishwasher.

○ Set a timer for longer, twenty minutes, to get some "desk work" done, such as paying bills, calendaring, or going through e-mails.

○ Pick just one item from your to-do list to do today. This is better than doing nothing. And at least you will be able to check one item off your list.

○ Tell yourself you won't leave the house until you have done "x" task.

○ Play the Fast Cleanup game with your children to see how quickly you can put away toys, books, games, and supplies. Or see who can put away the most in a set amount of time.

○ Give yourself a break for a set amount of time, twenty to thirty minutes or an hour. Set a timer or an alarm. Afterward, take care of at least one item. Plan incentives to look forward to each day or to reward yourself for finishing a specific task:

  ▪ Have lunch with a friend.

  ▪ Call a friend or a relative to talk.

  ▪ Implement short afternoon or evening rituals, varying them by season. This is welcome downtime and a pleasant break to look forward to each day.

PART THREE
MANAGE INFORMATION

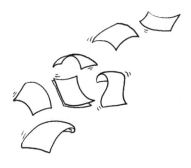

MANAGE INFORMATION

Information and requirements—the need for decisions to be made, action to be taken, and follow-up to be done—are like the tides. They flow in and out of our family homes regularly. As families, we use and generate a lot of information during the course of each day. We need this information to guide us on our way, but we also need to control it so we don't become engulfed by it. There are two main things to know in order to manage information effectively.

1. Know *what* information to gather. There is a lot of information we need for our families. Having the right information, the necessary information, makes our lives easier and allows us to make informed decisions. I've gathered the necessary information and summarized it in tables: *Family Reference Information Tables*. These tables and explanations for each are presented below and in Chapter Eight.

2. We need to know *how* to store the information so we have it when we need it. Some information you'll want to have available quickly and easily. Other information is important to keep, but you don't need to see it frequently.

To clarify how to save information, we can define the information by *type*, based on how quickly we need the information, how often we need the information, and how long we need to keep the information. There are three types of Reference Information:

1. Quick Reference: This is information that you need often and want to be able to access easily and quickly. (Examples: frequently used phone numbers or a roster for your child's current team, activity, or class.)

2. Current-Term Reference: This is information you need to save for current activities, organizations, or the school term. (Example: list of rules or guidelines for your child's current activity, current volunteer opportunities at your child's school or activity.) This information is good to keep but doesn't need to be readily available. You won't need to keep it once the current period is over.

3. Long-Term Reference: This is information that you keep indefinitely, past the current time period. (Example: rosters for your child's class, activity, school, and team.)

You'll notice in the above explanation of Reference Information Types that rosters begin as Quick Reference Information and later become Long-Term Reference Information.

This is because rosters have information that is useful to keep once the season or school year is finished for long-term reference; for example, addresses, parents' names and contact information, and more.

(You can find more information on saving and using Types of Reference Information in the Appendix.)

The following tables of *Family Reference Information* are included in this chapter:

1. *Family Health Care*
2. *Household and Auto—Service and Maintenance Providers*
3. *School and Activities Information*
4. *Social, Entertaining, and Vacations (optional)*

☆ FAMILY HEALTH CARE

Family Reference Information—Table One, shown below, lists the information to gather and keep up-to-date. It consists of: *Providers* of health care and your family's health care *Records*.

- **Providers** are the health professionals (doctors, dentists, and the like) and insurance companies, hospitals, and pharmacists that provide care, insurance coverage, and medication for your family. Gather this information to store in your Contacts app so you can access it easily and create an Emergency Reference Guide with this information to post in your home. You'll see this information in the Table as *Quick Reference Information*.
- **Records** consist of your child's immunizations, the notes that you take at doctor appointments, and any

research you do, as well as prescription information, insurance coverage, and insurance claims. This information doesn't need to be readily available. It consists of records that you'll want to keep for the current period (one year or less) or for a longer period. You'll see this information in the table as *Current-Term Reference Information* and *Long-Term Reference Information*. (Many health insurance providers have websites or apps that you can log into to access insurance coverage, insurance claims, and prescription information.)

FAMILY REFERENCE INFORMATION—TABLE ONE
FAMILY HEALTH CARE AND INSURANCE—PROVIDERS,
HEALTH AND PRESCRIPTIONS RECORDS

Types of Reference Information to Save

○ **Quick-Reference Information** should be saved where it can be accessed quickly and easily in your Smartphone Contacts app, Notes app, Calendar, or as a separate physical or online summary document.

○ **Current-Term Reference Information** is information you'll need occasionally during the current period.

○ **Long-Term Reference Information** should be saved indefinitely for reference.

Create separate Health-Care Records files for each family member to save with information such as immunization records, your notes from health-care appointments, research, and prescriptions information. You can create files online or use physical notebooks and/or files to store this information.

HEALTH-CARE PROVIDERS

○ **Doctors**
- Pediatrician, Pediatric Nurse(s), Office Manager
- Pediatric Dentist
- OB/GYN
- Family Primary Care Doctor
- Dentist
- Other Doctors
- Names of Assistants, Nurses, Office Managers

○ **Pharmacy**

○ **Prescription Service**

○ **After Hours Emergency Care Facility**

CONTACT INFO, WEBSITES, AND APPS

Quick Reference Info

○ **Doctor, Dentist, Pharmacy, After Hours/Urgent Care, Hospital, Insurance Company Providers:**
- Business Phone Numbers
- After Hours Phone Numbers
- E-mail Addresses
- Street Addresses
- Emergency Reference Guide (See the Emergency Reference Guide form in the Appendix. Create your

(continued on next page) ▶

▶ *(continued from previous page)*

○ **Hospital**

○ **Poison Control Phone Numbers**

own guide by filling in your providers' information as shown.) Post this Guide in your home for babysitters and other caregivers.

○ **Providers' Websites and Apps**
Most doctors, health practices, and hospitals offer patient portal websites or apps that allow you to access your health records, send notes to your doctor, and schedule appointments, using a secure login.

MEDICAL/DENTAL INSURANCE PROVIDERS

Quick Reference Info

- Name of Insurance Company
- Main Insurance Plan Identification Number(s)
- Family Members' ID numbers

○ **Contact Info**
- Business Phone Numbers
- E-mail Addresses

○ **Providers' Websites and Apps**
Most insurance companies have websites and apps with online access for their customers. These allow you to review your insurance claims, billing, reimbursement information, and more, using a user ID and password.

- Bookmark provider websites.
- Bookmark portal websites.
- Download all available provider apps.

- Bookmark provider websites.

- Bookmark patient portal websites.

- Download all available provider apps.

- Save user IDs and login passwords for websites and apps.

MEDICAL/DENTAL INSURANCE COVERAGE INFORMATION

Current-Term Reference Info

It's important to know your insurance coverage terms: what your insurance covers, the cost, your deductible and co-pay amounts, and more. You should be able to find this information by logging into

(continued on next page) ▶

▶ *(continued from previous page)*

- Save user IDs and login passwords for websites and apps.

O **Medical and Dental Insurance Cards**
Bring these cards to health-care visits. They show the insurance plan and family member ID numbers, as well as the insurance company contact information.

your insurance company website. (Note 1)

Open enrollment for health insurance happens annually, usually in November. This is the time to review insurance options for your family.

Of course, when your new baby arrives, you'll want to be sure to add her to your health insurance right away. (Note 2)

Notes

1. For more information on Health Insurance coverage, see: Understanding Your Health Insurance Policy on thebalance.com. www.thebalance.com/understanding-health-insurance-policy-2645652#help-%20 understandingyour-health-%20 insurance-policy-basics)

2. Adding your baby to your health insurance plan: Call your insurance company to add coverage for your baby. Some insurance companies will want a social security number and a copy of the baby's birth certificate. See: Checklist for Adding a Baby to Health Insurance on the budgeting. thenest.com website (https:// budgeting.thenest.com/checklist-adding-baby-health-insurance-life-insurance-24159.html)

(continued on next page) ▶

▶ (continued from previous page)

HEALTH RECORDS

Current and Long-Term Reference Info

○ **IMMUNIZATION RECORDS**
For a printable immunization schedule, go to: www.cdc.gov/vaccines/parents/downloads/milestones-tracker.pdf

○ **NOTES**
(See Appendix for Health-Care Visit Notes form.)
Save notes (as needed) from appointments and conversations with doctors, dentists, specialists, etc.

○ **RESEARCH INFO**
Keep information you've collected or gathered through research for relevant health or medical conditions.

PRESCRIPTIONS*	PRESCRIPTIONS RENEWALS	PRESCRIPTIONS HISTORY
Current-Term Reference Information	Enter the following in your Personal Calendar:	**Long-Term Reference Information**
■ Medication Name	■ Enter all prescription renewal dates in your calendar.	■ Medication Name
■ Medication Dosage		■ Medication Dosage
■ Prescription #	■ Schedule a follow-up doctor appointment if a renewal prescription is needed.*	■ Dates Taken
■ Pharmacy and Address		■ Notes—reason for taking
■ Prescribing Doctor		
■ Instructions and Precautions	* Schedule the follow-appointment before you leave the doctor's office, if possible, or ask for a reminder notice. If neither of these is possible, then set a reminder in your calendar to book the follow-up appointment.	
■ Refills (if applicable)		
■ When to Renew (if applicable)		
* Most of this information will be on the prescription label or related material that you get from the pharmacy.		

☆ HOUSEHOLD AND AUTO—SERVICE AND MAINTENANCE PROVIDERS

Maintaining a household and fulfilling your family's daily needs are a lot of work and responsibility. You'll use many services, have a number of accounts, and need to save various records. Discuss these responsibilities with your spouse or partner to decide which of these services and accounts you'd each like to keep track of and manage. *Family Reference Information—Table Two,* shown below, lists the information to gather and keep up-to-date. It consists of:

- **Service and Maintenance Providers:** These are auto service and repair businesses; providers of household utilities, maintenance, and repair; your landlord, if you are renting a home or apartment; subscriptions; and all the other miscellaneous programs and numbers you need to keep track of (airline frequent flyer numbers, rewards programs, etc.).

- **Records:** This category shows the records you need to save for current-term reference and provides a list of important information to save for long-term reference. It also lists frequently used numbers to have available for quick reference.

FAMILY REFERENCE INFORMATION—TABLE TWO
HOUSEHOLD AND AUTO—SERVICE MAINTENANCE PROVIDERS

Types of Reference Information to Save

○ **Quick Reference Information** should be saved where it can be accessed quickly and easily in your smartphone Contacts app, Notes app, Calendar, or as a separate physical or online summary document.

○ **Current-Term Reference Information** is information you'll need occasionally during the current period.

○ **Long-Term Reference Information** should be saved indefinitely for reference.

SERVICES AND MAINTENANCE PROVIDERS (as applicable)	CONTACT INFO, WEBSITES, AND APPS FOR PROVIDERS
○ **Utilities** 　■ Gas 　■ Electric 　■ Water 　■ Phone - Landline 　■ Phone - Mobile/Cell 　■ Trash Service 　■ Cable 　■ Wi-fi ○ **Subscriptions** 　■ Digital and Print 　■ Newspapers 　■ Magazines ○ **Entertainment Accounts** 　■ Streaming Services 　■ Others ○ **Loyalty Rewards Programs** 　■ Airlines 　■ Retail 　■ Other ○ **Repesentative/Landlord for Rental Home or Apartment**	**Quick Reference Info** Save the following for each provider (as needed): 　○ Account Name/Number 　○ Account Representative 　○ Phone Numbers 　○ E-mail Address 　○ Street/Mailing Address 　○ Download available apps. 　○ Bookmark websites. 　○ Websites and Apps Access Info; User IDs and Login Passwords **OTHER IMPORTANT NUMBERS** **Quick Reference Info** Create a list of the numbers shown below: 　○ Social Security Numbers (for each family member) 　○ Drivers' License Numbers (for each family member) 　○ Car(s) License Plate Number(s)

(continued on next page) ▶

▶ *(continued from previous page)*

○ **Home Repair and Appliance Services**

○ **House Cleaning Services**

○ **Auto Service**

AUTO RECORDS	RENTAL HOME OR APARTMENT RECORDS
Current-Term Reference Info	**Current-Term Reference Info**
○ Lease or Finance Records	○ Rental Documents
Long-Term Reference Info	
○ Service Records	
○ Title (Pink Slip) if owned—Keep original title(s) in safe deposit box or other secure location	

OWNED HOME RECORDS

Quick Reference Info

○ Note the real estate tax due dates in your personal calendar. Example: April 10 and December 10

○ Make a note in your calendar or schedule a reminder ten days prior to the due dates for your semiannual real estate taxes to avoid a late payment penalty. Example: April 1 and December 1

Current-Term Reference Info

○ Semiannual real estate tax bills: Keep these where you can access them easily.

Long-Term Reference Info

○ Mortgage loan documents

○ Appraisal (if you have one)

○ Real estate improvements and substantial repair cost records

○ Title to home, if you have no mortgage—Keep original title in safe deposit box or other secure location.

☆ SCHOOL AND ACTIVITIES

Family Reference Information—Table Three, shown below, lists the information to gather and keep up-to-date. It consists of: School and Activities Contact Information, School Calendar and Activities Schedules, and Additional Information.

- **School and Activities Contact Information:** Once your child enters school and has activities, you'll want to have the contact information for these readily available by entering them into your smartphone Contacts app.
- **School Calendar and Activities Schedules:** You'll also want to enter school calendar dates and activity scheduled dates in your personal calendar.
- **Additional Information:** Websites, Rosters, Class Curriculum and Guidelines, Schedule of Classes, Other
  - *Schedule of Classes:* Once your child is in middle school, she will have a varied schedule with multiple teachers and classrooms. I found it helpful to have this information consolidated, showing:
    - Class period and days each class meets
    - Teachers' contact info
    - Teachers' website (if any) and access info
  - *Daily Bell Schedule:* The daily bell schedule will usually appear in the student directory or on the school website. It can vary based on the number of classes meeting each day, and for minimum days, teacher days, administration days, teacher conferences, and more.
  - *Rosters:* Rosters for school and activities are invaluable. Study these so you know your child's friends, classmates,

and fellow activity participants. Always save rosters. Knowing your child's classmates, friends, and others he associates with is an important part of understanding and being part of your child's world. Rosters tell you children's names, their parents' names, their contact information, and their addresses. This knowledge can help you put a car pool together, arrange playdates, and feel comfortable talking with other children and parents because you can greet them by name. If a roster is not available, you can make one by gathering the necessary information. Give copies to other parents. I did this several times. Parents appreciate the information. It is easier to connect with one another when you know everyone's names. Your time spent together may result in friendships as you sit together during your child's sport season, arts performance, or other activities, especially if your child continues in the same sport or activity over many years. Another good reason to have a roster is because children can look quite similar from your seat in the bleachers or audience, especially when they are wearing a uniform and have a similar build to your child. It's easy to confuse one for the other. I found myself cheering for the "wrong" child on more than one occasion when I mistook another child for my own.

- Class Curriculum, Activity Guidelines, Other: Hold on to any information you get from teachers, coaches, and administrators for the current school or activity period. This is useful information that gives insight into your child's learning and development.

FAMILY REFERENCE INFORMATION—TABLE THREE
SCHOOL AND ACTIVITIES

Types of Reference Information to Save

○ **Quick Reference Information** should be saved where it can be accessed quickly and easily in your smartphone Contact app, Notes app, Calendar, or as a separate physical or online summary document.

○ **Current-Term Reference Information** is information you'll need occasionally during the current period.

○ **Long-Term Reference Information** should be saved indefinitely for reference.

SCHOOL ADMINISTRATION:
CONTACT INFO AND WEBSITES

Store often-needed school information in your smartphone for:
○ School Attendance Phone Line
○ School Office
○ Bookmark websites.
○ Save website user IDs and login passwords.

SCHOOL DIRECTORY*

Current-Term Reference Info

Be sure to purchase/obtain the school directory. (Usually you will receive a directory when you pay for membership in the PTA.) It's helpful to keep an extra copy of the directory in your car. The directory includes:

○ **Contact Info for:**
- Administration and Teachers
- PTA
- Foundation (if applicable)
- Students and Parents

SCHOOL CALENDARS(S)

Personal Calendar Info

You may be able to download and/or sync the school calendar with your personal online calendar (if your school makes it available). If not, enter the school calendar dates shown below into your

Personal Calendar:
○ Holidays
○ Teacher days
○ Minimum days

(continued on next page) ▶

▶ *(continued from previous page)*

- Other information
  - School Calendar
  - Bell Schedule for Classes
  - Other

  * Save the directory at the end of the school year for Long-Term Reference.

○ Altered-schedule days
○ Beginning and ending grading period dates
○ Exam schedule dates (if applicable)

SCHOOL TEACHERS: CONTACT INFO AND WEBSITES

Quick Reference Info

Include the following information in contact info for each teacher:

○ Teacher's Name
○ Notes: Include preferred method of contact.
○ Phone Number
○ E-mail Address
○ Bookmark websites.
○ Save user IDs and login passwords.

SCHOOL CLASS INFO

Current-Term Reference Info

○ Class Curriculum
○ Class Guidelines
○ Class Info and Teacher Handouts
○ Schedule of Classes (beginning in middle school, when children have more than one teacher)
○ School Directory*
○ Class Roster*

* Save the School Directory and Class Roster at the end of the school year for Long-Term Reference.

ACTIVITIES: CONTACT INFO AND WEBSITES

Quick Reference Info

Include the following information in contact info for each activity:

○ Activity Name
○ Address
○ Phone Number
○ E-mail Address
○ Coach/Teacher Name

ACTIVITY SCHEDULE

Personal Calendar

○ Schedule - Input all schedule information

ACTIVITY INFORMATION

Current-Term Reference Info

○ Rules for Class or Team

ACTIVITY CAR POOL

(if applicable)

Quick Reference Info

○ Car Pool Participants
○ Home Addresses
○ Phone Numbers
○ E-mail Addresses

(continued on next page) ▶

▶ *(continued from previous page)*

○ Notes: Include preferred method of contact
○ Bookmark websites.
○ Save user IDs and login passwords.

○ Requirements for Parent Participatiion or Volunteer Opportunities

ACTIVITY ROSTER*

Current-Term Reference Info

Bring the roster to games, performances, practices, etc. If one is not available, you can make and distribute it to parents. Include:

○ children's names and their parents' names
○ home addresses and phone numbers
○ children's corresponding uniform number, position, part, etc.

* After the activity ends, save the roster for Long-Term reference.

CAR POOL SCHEDULES

Personal Calendar

○ Input days and times assigned for each driver.
○ Note any guidelines you have agreed upon, such as providing snacks or assisting with changing clothes, shoes, etc.

☆ SOCIAL, ENTERTAINING, AND VACATIONS

Family Reference Information—Table Four, shown below, lists the information to gather and keep up-to-date. It consists of lists and notes.

- **Month-by-Month Dates to Remember List:** This list is helpful to have and save as quick reference. This way you can refer to it easily and know ahead of time when you need to get a gift or card, contact someone, or celebrate a special occasion.
- **Current-Year Gifts List:** This is a helpful list to make and save so you can remember what you got friends and family as well as avoid giving duplicate gifts.
- **Current-Year Holiday Card Recipients List:** If you send out a yearly holiday card, this list will save you from having to make a new list every year. You can add notes about recipients as useful reminders, for example: "Son, William, plays baseball; daughter, Christine, plays soccer."
- **Vacation and Entertaining Notes:** The notes I make on entertaining help me plan and prepare for each occasion. I began to keep notes on vacations and guests because at one point, I realized that I couldn't always remember when certain guests had visited or which years we had gone on certain trips. I enjoy looking back at these notes and remembering good times with family and friends.

You can store your lists and notes in an online folder or in a loose-leaf binder. I like to use small five-by-seven-inch notebooks. Add the current-year lists and notes to your binders or online files/folders at the end of each year to save for Long-Term Reference.

FAMILY REFERENCE INFORMATION—TABLE FOUR SOCIAL LISTS, ENTERTAINING, AND VACATIONS NOTES	
Reference Information to Save Create files online or use physical notebooks to save lists and notes. At the end of each year, add the current-year lists to the online folder or binder to save for Long-Term reference.	
SOCIAL LISTS	**VACATIONS AND ENTERTAINING NOTES**
<u>Quick Reference Info</u>	<u>Long-Term Reference</u>

○ **Month-By-Month Dates to Remember**
Create a Quick Reference Document for yearly occasions to remember.
 	
List by:
■ Date
■ Occasion
  - Birthday
  - Anniversary
  - Holiday
  - Other
 	
<u>Current-Term Reference Info</u>
 	
○ **Current-Year Gifts List**
  Include:
  ■ Date
  ■ Gift recipient name
	○ **Vacations**
	Include:
	■ Dates
	■ Location(s)
	■ Who went
	■ Notes on memorable moments and highlights
	○ **Entertaining Notes—(Hosted at home or away)**
	Make brief notes about each occasion. Include:
	■ A copy of the online invitation or physical invitation (if you sent one)
	■ The occasion (dinner with friends, birthday celebration, holiday), date, time, and place
	■ Guests' names
	■ Menu—list each course as applicable:
	  - Drinks before, during, and after meal
	  - Appetizers
	  - Soup or salad
	  - Main course
	  - Dessert

(continued on next page) ▶

▶ *(continued from previous page)*

- Gift description
- Occasion

○ **Current-Year Holiday Card Recipients List**
Create a group within your Contacts app or make a reference document. Include:
  - Names
  - Addresses
  - Notes (if any)

- **Preparation Notes**—List the steps that can be done ahead of time and when to do them.
- **Decor Notes**—flowers, decorations, or theme for your gathering
- **Post-event notes**—brief highlights

For Events Hosted at Home
Include:
  - Serving dishes and place settings—flatware, plates, bowls, glasses, etc.
  - Recipes—Note where to find each.
  - Grocery list of ingredients to buy
  - Catered or prepared foods (if applicable). Note where and when to pick up.

○ **House Guest Notes**
Make brief notes about your guests' visit. Include:
  - Guests' names
  - Dates of visit
  - Notes on outings and activities

There will always be much for you to do and manage. I hope the suggestions, organizing tips, and tables of information in this chapter will help you. Remember to keep it simple, take it one step at a time, and give yourself credit for doing the best you can.

My wish is that you are able to share responsibilities and tasks within your family and find comfortable rhythms in the routine ways you manage your household. May your home hum with harmony and hold the warmth of your steady care.

In Chapter Eight:

FAMILY FINANCES AND SAFEGUARDS

(your baby/child will be referred to

as "he" or "she" alternately)

- Importance of Budgeting, Financial Planning, Implementing Safeguards, and Investing for Your Family
- Sample Monthly Budget
- Family Reference Information Tables—(continued from Chapter Seven)
  5. Household Budget and Bill Paying
  6. Financial Accounts, Insurance Policies, and Taxes
  7. Safeguards: Estate Planning, Insurance, and Important Documents

Chapter Eight

FAMILY FINANCES
AND SAFEGUARDS

Once your beautiful baby comes into your world, budgeting, financial planning, safeguards, and investing will take on greater importance. You will realize the need to be responsible for your baby and to plan for her future.

Putting together your financial plan and creating safeguards for your child is a process that will take time. It will require consideration, research, and may include working with an attorney and a financial advisor. Take it all step by step. You'll want to name guardians for your child, draw up a will, and possibly put a revocable living trust in place and increase your life insurance. (More on these later in this chapter.)

☆ HOUSEHOLD BUDGET AND BILL PAYING

Start by making a monthly budget, tied to your goals and plans for your family's future. To create your budget, talk with

CREATING A BUDGET

○ Discuss your financial goals with your partner or spouse.

○ Determine any immediate large purchase needs.

○ Determine your long-term savings goals.

○ Create your budget to align with your income and your spending and savings goals.

your spouse or partner. Consider questions such as: Do you have immediate large purchases or spending priorities such as buying a new car? Do you need to furnish your house or apartment? If you want to buy a house, how much do you need to save for a down payment? Other financial questions you may have: Can you begin to save money for your child's college education? What kind of vacation would you like to take? How much do you need to save for vacation? Answering these questions will help you clarify your spending and savings goals. After you have answered these questions, look at your goals and decide which ones you would like to prioritize.

Next, look at your income and spending. List your monthly income and fixed expenses such as your home, utilities, gas, car, student loans, food, sundries, and other household expenses. Work on your budget to align your spending and savings to meet your goals. A sample budget could look like this:

SAMPLE MONTHLY BUDGET
For a Family with a Net Income of $4000 Each Month

Semimonthly Net Income Received on 15th of each Month = $2000		Semimonthly Net Income Received on 30th of each Month = $2000	
Monthly Expenses/Bills:	Bills to Pay on the 15th	Monthly Expenses/Bills:	Bills to Pay on the 30th
▪ Utilities (1)	$200	▪ Mortgage/ Rent Payment	$1,500
▪ Monthly Cash/ Entertainment (2)	$300	▪ Auto Payment(s)	$300
▪ Food, Sundries, Gas (3)	$500	▪ Household Expenses (4)	$200
▪ Student/Other Loans/ Credit Cards	$200	**Total Expenses to Pay on the 30th**	**$2,000**
Total Expenses to Pay on the 15th	**$1,200**		
Savings	$800	Savings	$0

Monthly Savings = $800	Annual Savings = $9,600
Save $400 Monthly for Yearly Expenses (5)	$4,800—Yearly Expenses $400 x 12 = $4,800 (5)
Save $400 Monthly for Long-Term Goals (6)	$4,800—Long-Term Goals $400 x 12 = $4,800 (6)

Notes

(1) Utility Costs: These costs will vary from month to month. Set an average amount in your budget. If utilities cost less than the set amount in one month, then roll the extra amount to the next month. If in another month, utilities cost more than the set amount, use money rolled from prior months to cover that month's higher cost. Adjust the average set amount as needed.

(2) Monthly Cash/Entertainment: It's easy to lose track of cash and entertainment spending. This is an important category to monitor.

(3) Food, Sundries, and Gas: These costs will vary (similar to utility costs). Set an average amount in your budget to manage your spending and adjust as necessary.

(continued on next page) ▶

▶ *(continued from previous page)*

(4) Household Expenses: Repairs, maintenance, etc. will vary from month to month. Again, set an average amount in your budget and adjust as needed.

(5) Yearly Expense Savings: Use these savings to cover your large expenses that aren't monthly recurring costs. Large expenses include insurance premiums, vacation, real estate taxes (if applicable), big purchases or expenses such as home projects, furniture, and more.

(6) Savings for Long-Term Goals: These are annual savings that you will add to each year to fund your long-term goals such as a down payment for a home, college savings account(s), retirement account(s), etc.

Set up your monthly budget so your bill paying corresponds to when you are paid. For example, if you are on salary, you will be paid twice a month. This makes it easy to schedule your bill payments twice a month, as shown in the sample budget above. Look at your actual bills and expenses a couple times each month to see how your spending aligns with your budget. Stay on track and aware of your goals by reviewing, adjusting, and revising your budget as needed.

You'll find many resources online to guide you in making a budget. I've included a website that provides budgeting guidance in the table below.

Family Reference Information—Table Five, shown below, has guidelines for budgeting, saving, and paying your bills.

- **Budget:** Your budget shows your income, expenses, and savings.
- **Bill Paying:** The bill paying information shows you how to simplify this task. Start by automating your payments as much as possible. Do this by using Routine

Payment Methods. Find out which service providers allow you to pay monthly bills with an automatic charge to your credit card or an automatic debit to your checking account. Authorize these charges or debits with all companies that offer this payment option. (Be sure to pay off these monthly credit card charges each month to avoid interest charges.) Schedule other bill payments on the 15th or the 30th of each month through online banking. Remember to record and verify these transactions each month.

FAMILY REFERENCE INFORMATION—TABLE FIVE
HOUSEHOLD BUDGET AND BILL PAYING

Budget Guidelines

Determine your household budget by adding all monthly income and subtracting your expected monthly expenses. (*See: Sample Monthly Budget*, on page 189.) Remember to plan for annual expenses. Save funds each month by setting up automatic transfers of money from your checking account to your savings or investment accounts.

You can find additional financial guidance and a worksheet in the website below:

○ **kiplinger.com**
○ **Household Budget Worksheet** (www.kiplinger.com/kiplinger-tools/spending/t007-s001-budgeting-worksheet-a-household-budget-for-today-a/index.php)

HOUSEHOLD BUDGET	BILL PAYING
Save your budget as a Quick Reference Document to refer to each month when paying your bills. Store it in the Notes app of your smartphone or, if you use a paper calendar, by placing a physical copy in there.	Pay your bills on time by using one or more of the following Routine Payment Methods: ❖ Automatic Payments: ▪ Arrange monthly automatic debits from your

(continued on next page) ▶

▶ *(continued from previous page)*

○ **Monthly Income**
  ▪ Sources

○ **Monthly Expenses**
  ▪ Mortgage or rent payment
  ▪ Groceries, personal and household care products
  ▪ Gas
  ▪ Auto payment(s)
  ▪ Student loans
  ▪ Utilities
  ▪ Activity costs
  ▪ Monthly membership fees
  ▪ Subscriptions
  ▪ Housecleaning and garden maintenance
  ▪ Entertainment
  ▪ Clothing
  ▪ Gifts
  ▪ Other

○ **Monthly Savings**
  ▪ Arrange monthly automatic transfers from your checking account for the amount you want to save each month.

checking account for bill payments.

  ▪ Arrange monthly automatic charges to your credit card for bill payments. (Pay off these monthly credit card charges each month to avoid interest charges.)

❖ Schedule specific bill payments on the same day each month. Example: on the 15th and 30th of the month

❖ Pay all other bills as soon as you receive them by mail or e-mail. (This way you deal with these bills just once.)

❖ Note bill payment due dates on your calendar with reminder notices. (Use this method if you do not use automatic or scheduled payments.)

☆ FINANCIAL ACCOUNTS, INSURANCE POLICIES, AND TAXES

It's important to have a complete and up-to-date list of your financial and insurance accounts, where they are held, and the contact and access information for each. *Family Reference Information—Table Six* shows the information to gather for your financial assets, financial liabilities, and the insurance that protects your assets. It also shows the information to gather for handling your taxes.

FAMILY REFERENCE INFORMATION—TABLE SIX

FINANCIAL ACCOUNTS, INSURANCE POLICIES, AND TAXES

Types of Reference Information to Save

O **Quick Reference Information** should be saved where it can be accessed quickly and easily in your smartphone Contacts app, Notes app, Calendar, or as a separate physical or online summary document.

O **Current-Term Reference Information** is information you'll need occasionally during the current period.*

O **Long-Term Reference Information** should be saved indefinitely for reference.*

* Create files online or use physical notebooks and/or files to store this information.

FINANCIAL ACCOUNTS	FINANCIAL ACCOUNTS: CONTACT INFO, WEBSITES, AND APPS
O **Assets** ▪ Checking Accounts (See Records, Note 1) ▪ Savings Accounts ▪ Investment Accounts	**Quick Reference Info** Save the following for your financial accounts company providers:

(continued on next page) ▶

▶ *(continued from previous page)*

○ **Liabilities**
- Credit Cards (Note 1)
- Loans (Note 2)
- Home Mortgage (Note 2)
- Auto Loans/Leases (Note 2)
- Lines of Credit (Note 2)

Notes

1. Create a list of automatic monthly charges to your checking accounts and credit cards (if any), e.g., health club fees, utilities, subscriptions. Save this list for <u>Current-term reference</u>. Be sure to update automatic payment accounts when you receive a new or replacement card.

2. Keep a copy of loan documents or create a Summary Document for each loan with the following information:

- Loan Amount
- Loan Origination Date
- Loan Interest Rate
- Loan Due Date
- Monthly Payment Date
- Monthly Payment Amount

Save this information for <u>Current-term Reference</u>.

- Account Representative
- Phone Numbers
- Account Name
- Account Number
- Account Type
- Download available apps.
- Bookmark website.
- Websites and Apps Access Info; User IDs and Login Passwords
- E-mail Address
- Street/Mailing Address

(continued on next page) ▶

▶ *(continued from previous page)*

INSURANCE POLICY ACCOUNTS	INSURANCE ACCOUNTS: CONTACT INFO, WEBSITES, AND APPS	INSURANCE RECORDS
○ **Life Insurance** (Note 3) ○ **Auto Insurance** (Note 4) ○ **Home or Renter's Insurance** ○ **Other Insurance** ○ **Umbrella Policy** ○ **Flood Insurance** ○ **Earthquake Insurance** ○ **Home or Renter's Insurance** ○ **Additional Riders** (Note 5)	**Quick Reference Info** Save the following: ■ Agent Representative ■ Phone Numbers ■ E-mail Address ■ Street/Mailing Address (if needed) ■ Download available apps ■ Bookmark website. ■ Website and App Access Info; User IDs and Login Passwords	**Current-Term Reference Info** Save or know how to access the following information online: ○ Declarations Page for each insurance policy. This shows: ■ Type of Policy (home, auto, life, etc.) ■ Policy Number ■ Policy Term— dates the policy is in effect ■ Insurance Amount ■ Premium cost of insurance policy ■ Deductible— the amount you pay before you receive

Notes—(cont.)

3. Life Insurance: You and your spouse/partner may want to increase your life insurance before or soon after your baby is born. (See Table Seven for further discussion of life insurance.)

4. Auto Insurance: You'll need to bring a copy of your auto insurance declaration page when you volunteer to drive for a school trip.

(continued on next page) ▶

▶ *(continued from previous page)*

5. Extra insurance riders insure your extra-valuable property such as jewelry, antiques, electronics, etc. Save your purchase receipts/ documentation and/ or appraisals for these to provide evidence of their value.

reimbursement from the insurance company when you report a loss

TAX SERVICES— CONTACT INFO, WEBSITES, AND APPS

Quick Reference Info

○ **Tax Accountant**
○ **Bookeeper**
○ **Other**

Extra Save the following for the above tax service providers:

- Phone Numbers
- E-mail Address
- Street/Mailing Address
- Download available apps (if applicable)
- Bookmark websites (if applicable)
- Save websites and apps access info, user IDs and login passwords (if applicable)

TAX RECORDS*

Current and Long-Term Reference Info

Current-Term Reference Records
Save all tax-related receipts and documents that you accumulate throughout the year in a current-year tax collection file. These will be needed to prepare your annual tax returns.

- Receipts/records for deductible purchases or charitable donations
- Income and expense records for personal business, partnerships, etc.
- Year-end financial and investment account statements
- W-2(s)
- Tax statements from financial investments, insurance, real estate taxes, mortgage interest, etc.

(continued on next page) ▶

▶ *(continued from previous page)*

	Long-Term Reference Records Save the following: ▪ Annual State Tax Returns ▪ Annual Federal Tax Returns * To find out how long you need to keep tax-related records, go to the IRS website page: "How Long Should I Keep Records?" (www.irs.gov/ businesses/small-businesses-self-employed/how-long-should-i-keep-records)

☆ SAFEGUARDS: ESTATE PLANNING, INSURANCE, AND IMPORTANT DOCUMENTS

As the parent of a minor child, it's important to have a plan in place for the worst-case scenario—that you or your spouse die prematurely, or you both die, leaving your child without parents. You and your spouse or partner can provide for your child by purchasing life insurance for both of you. You'll each want to name one another as beneficiary, not your child, because naming a minor as a beneficiary can cause delays for your child in obtaining funds from the policy. If you want to name your child as the beneficiary, you'll need to set up a transfer of the insurance policy into a custodial trust under the UTMA (Uniform Transfer to Minors Act) or the UGMA (Uniform Gift to Minors Act), depending on which state you live in. The insurance agent can assist you with setting up this type of account.

You can also provide for your child by executing two basic documents of estate planning. These are a will and a revocable trust (aka living trust.) Your will names your child's guardian(s), names an executor for your will, and states how you want your assets (property) to be distributed after you die.

The executor will settle your finances, pay any debts and taxes owed, and distribute the remaining assets to the heirs you specified in your will. Without a will, it will be up to the courts to name a guardian(s) for your child.

A revocable trust establishes a trust to place your assets in. If you are just starting out and haven't accumulated assets, you may not need to set up a trust at this point. See the website uslegalforms.com (https://www.uslegalforms.com/ livingtrusts/why-living-trust-are-important.htm) to learn the advantages of having a trust. You can continue to manage your assets by naming yourself and/or your spouse or part-ner trustee. You'll need to name a trustee(s) to manage the trust when you die. Having a trust allows your heirs to avoid the lengthy and often expensive probate process. The distri-bution of your assets is kept private because trust assets are disbursed outside of the public process of probate.

Estate planning is essential for parents of minor children. I have included two websites with information to help you understand the basic safeguards you can put in place for your child in Table Seven, shown below. It's fairly straightforward to execute a simple will and to establish a custodian account with life insurance with your child as beneficiary under the UTMA or UGMA laws. You might decide to use legal forms that you fill out and execute yourself. However, you'll want to be sure the documents are applicable for your personal circumstances by working with an attorney. Wills and revo-cable trusts can be updated when, and as often as, you like.

We were very late in doing our estate planning. I remem-ber talking with my sister and her husband about taking care of our children, but we didn't formally designate them until we had an attorney draft a simple will and living trust when our daughter was in kindergarten. Happily, the "worst" had not occurred, and our children did not need to go through the courts to have their futures decided.

The last table of *Family Reference Information—Table Seven*, is shown below. It summarizes the information to have and save for your estate planning and includes other original documents you'll want to keep track of.

When you are able, discuss with your spouse or partner your finances and goals to determine your budget. Automate

---

FAMILY REFERENCE INFORMATION—TABLE SEVEN
SAFEGUARDS: ESTATE PLANNING,
INSURANCE, AND IMPORTANT DOCUMENTS

Types of Reference Information to Save

○ **Quick Reference Information** should be saved where it can be accessed quickly and easily in your smartphone Contacts app, Notes app, Calendar, or as a separate physical or online summary document.
○ **Current-Term Reference Information** is information you'll need occasionally during the current period.*
○ **Long-Term Reference Information** should be saved indefinitely for reference.*

* Create files online or use physical notebooks and/or files to store this information.

ESTATE PLANNING INFORMATION AND INSURANCE

A simple will and living trust will protect and provide for your minor child or children in the unlikely event that you or your spouse dies prematurely or both of you die prematurely. You can find more information on estate planning at the website thebalance.com (https://www.thebalance.com/estate-planning-4073957). Review the information under Estate Planning Basics.

(continued on next page) ▶

▶ *(continued from previous page)*

WILL*

The most important reason for having a will is that it names the guardian(s) you have chosen to raise your minor child or children. It also states how your assets will be distributed when you die.

REVOCABLE (LIVING) TRUST AGREEMENT*

The benefit of having a trust is that it allows your child or children to avoid the lengthy probate process that would occur without having it in place. It also keeps information about the assets and their distribution private.

> * Keep the originals in your safe deposit box or other secure location. Be sure a trusted family member or an advisor knows where to locate these. Keep a copy of each document at home for Current-Term Reference.

LIFE INSURANCE

Term life insurance is an effective and simple way to provide for your minor child. You and your spouse should name one another as beneficiary. If you want to name your child as your beneficiary, you will need to open a custodial account under the UTMA or UGMA law (depending on your state residency) to do so. See the website Policygenius.com (www.policygenius.com/life-insurance/life-insurance-for-new-parents/#when-should-new-parents-buy-life-insurance) to find answers to the questions new parents have about buying insurance.

ESTATE PLANNING & INSURANCE CONTACT INFO, WEBSITES, AND APPS

- ○ **Children's Guardian(s)**
- ○ **Executor(s) for Will**
- ○ **Attorney Who Drafted Will**
- ○ **Attorney Who Drafted Trust**
- ○ **Trustees for Trust—** (if applicable)
- ○ **Insurance Policy Representative**

ADDITIONAL ORIGINAL LEGAL DOCUMENTS*

<u>**Current-Term Reference Info**</u>

Make copies of the following:

- ○ **Birth Certificates**
- ○ **Adoption Decree** (if applicable)
- ○ **Marriage Certificate**
- ○ **Passports**

(continued on next page) ▶

▶ *(continued from previous page)*

Quick Reference Info

Save the following for the individuals shown above:

- ⭘ Phone Numbers
- ⭘ E-mail Addresses
- ⭘ Home and Business Addresses
- ⭘ Bookmark websites.
- ⭘ Website Access Info; User IDs and Password
- ⭘ Website Portal(s) Access Info; User IDs and Login Passwords (if applicable)

- ⭘ **Social Security Cards** (if available)
- ⭘ **Title to Home** (if no mortgage)
- ⭘ **Title to Auto** (if no loan)

* Keep originals in your safe deposit box or other secure location.

your bill paying and savings as much as possible. Gather your financial, insurance, and tax information to save as needed. Use the Family Reference Information tables to guide you in saving the information you need for each category. Try to keep your information up-to-date as much as possible.

Talk with your spouse or partner about whom you would like to choose as guardian(s) for your child or children and be sure they agree. Execute a will that states your intentions and put financial protections in place as you see fit to provide safeguards for your child or children.

Each of these tasks is considerable but meaningful. Sticking to a budget and managing finances are a challenge that will require discipline. Congratulations on determining your financial goals, putting safeguards in place, and following through with the hard work it takes to reach your goals. I wish you the very best in your endeavors and your determination.

In Chapter Nine: RESOURCES

RESOURCES FROM CHAPTERS ONE-EIGHT
- Chapter One: The First Three Months
- Chapter Two: Four Months to One Year
- Chapter Three: Age One
- Chapter Four: Ages Two and Three
- Chapter Five: Ages Three to Five—Preschool Years
- Chapter Six: Age Range: Four to Six—Kindergarten
- Chapter Seven: Family Organizatioin
- Chapter Eight: Family Finances and Safeguards

RESOURCES BY CATEGORY AND ADDITIONAL RESOURCES
- Family Health and Wellness
  - Healthy Living
  - General Health Information
  - Mom's Health Concerns
  - Health Insurance
- Parent Education
  - Children's Temperament
  - Children's Development
  - Attention and Learning Concerns
- Building Community and Volunteering
  - Mothers' Organizations
  - School Volunteering
- Children's Education
  - Preschool
  - Kindergarten
- Mothers' Employment and Careers
  - Articles
  - Books
- Media and Social Media Guidelines
  - General Information
- Family Finances and Safeguards
  - Budgeting
  - Taxes
  - Estate Planning—Wills and Living Trusts
  - General Information
  - Life Insurance for Parents
- Organization
  - Calendar Options
  - Recipe Storage Options

Chapter Nine

RESOURCES BY CHAPTER

CHAPTER ONE: THE FIRST THREE MONTHS— BEGINNING DAYS OF MOTHERHOOD

○ **The Female Brain by Louann Brizendine, M.D.** {https://en.wikipedia.org/wiki/The_Female_Brain_(book)} discusses research on the transformations that occur in the brains of mothers, including adoptive mothers, to ensure the connection between mothers and their babies.

○ **Baby Blues and Postpartum Depression**

  ■ "Baby Blues or Postpartum Depression?" (www.babycenter.com/0_the-baby-blues_11704.bc)

  ■ "Postpartum Depression Guide" (www.webmd.com/depression/postpartum-depression/understanding-postpartum-depression-basics#1)

○ **Vaccination Records**

  ■ Printable immunization schedule (www.cdc.gov/vaccines/parents/downloads/milestones-tracker.pdf)

CHAPTER TWO: FOUR MONTHS TO ONE YEAR—ADAPTING TO NEW PRIORITIES AND ROUTINES

- ○ **Connect with Moms** (Additional Resources are included below in Mothers' Organizations under *Additional Resources by Category, Building Community and Volunteering.*)
  - ▪ Mothers' Organizations (www.karenbongiorno.com/it-takes-a-village): Scroll down to Mothers' Organizations. Use the following terms to search online for ways to connect with other mothers:
    - – mothers' clubs/groups
    - – working mothers' baby playgroups
    - – meet up mothers
    - – your town; mothers' groups
    - – new mothers' groups
- ○ **Mothers, Employment, and Career Navigation** (Reading: Articles and Books)
  - ▪ "The Open Secret of Anti-Mom Bias at Work," by Katherine Goldstein, *New York Times,* May 16, 2018.
  - ▪ "Upshot Letter: Our Anti-Parenting Bias," by David Leonhardt, *New York Times*, April 3, 2015.
  - ▪ "A Labor Market Punishing to Mothers," by David Leonhardt, *New York Times*, August 3, 2010.
  - ▪ "Two Jobs, Two New Parents: How to Negotiate Your New Reality," by Elissa Strauss, Parenting, *New York Times*, May 6, 2019.
  - ▪ *Forget "Having It All": How America Messed Up Motherhood—and How to Fix It,* by Amy Westervelt. New York, NY: Seal Press, 2018.
  - ▪ Additional Reading shown below in *Mothers, Employment, and Careers.*

CHAPTER THREE: AGE ONE—BEGINNING COMMUNITY

○ **Children's Growth and Development**

- Gesell Institute Studies (https://gesellinstitute.org): The Gesell Institute was founded in 1950 and has been dedicated to understanding children's growth and how it affects development. There are individual books for ages one through nine. Each is titled by age: *Your One-Year-Old, Your Two-Year-Old*, etc.

- "The Nine Temperament Traits" (https://childdevelopment info.com/child-development/temperament_and_your_child/temp2/#gs.kbyvkq)
  1. Activity Level
  2. Distractibility
  3. Intensity
  4. Regularity
  5. Sensory Threshold
  6. Approach/Withdrawal
  7. Adaptability
  8. Persistence
  9. Mood

CHAPTER FOUR: AGES TWO AND THREE— EARLY CHILDHOOD

○ **Preschool Research:** Preschools offer programs based on varying ideas. Often their approach may combine several theories. The resources shown here provide information on these differing philosophies.

- GreatSchools.org (www.greatschools.org/gk/?s=Pre-school%20philosophies) has several articles to help you consider different types of preschools, based on their varying philosophies. The articles explain how each type implements its approach to child development and learning.

- "Challenge Success: Do You Know?" (www.challenge success.org/resources/research/do-you-know/): This article from Challenge Success compiles research into a discussion of academic-based vs. play-based preschools.

- Limit screen time for your baby/child; commonsense-media.org (www.commonsensemedia.org/screen-time/how-much-screen-time-is-ok-for-my-kids) is an excellent resource for determining limits at every age.

CHAPTER FIVE: AGES THREE TO FIVE—PRESCHOOL YEARS

○ **Kindergarten Entrance Age**
  - "Education Commission of the States—50 State Comparison" (https://c0arw235.caspio.com/dp/b7f930007026a9cefb46435c95df)

CHAPTER SIX: AGE RANGE: FOUR TO SEVEN—KINDERGARTEN

○ **Kindergarten Learning**
  - "What Kids Learn in Kindergarten" (www.k5learning.com/blog/what-kids-learn-kindergarten): This article from the K5 Learning Blog gives an overview of what children learn in kindergarten.
  - "K5 Learning Worksheets" (www.k5learning.com/free-preschool-kindergarten-worksheets): This site has free downloadable worksheets for many different activities, offered by K5 Learning.

CHAPTER SEVEN: FAMILY ORGANIZATION

○ **Calendar Apps:** There are many calendar apps you can download to your smartphone to help you manage your family calendar. Below are two I like:

- Family Organizer by Sevenlogics (www.sevenlogics.com/): This mobile app allows you to record and keep track of your to-dos, recipes, and more. (The free version has advertising.)
- Iphone Week Cal (www.weekcal.com): I like the agenda view of this app for the iPhone.

○ **Recipe Organizing**

- Pinterest My Recipes (www.pinterest.com/myrecipes/): This site allows you to search, save, and organize recipes.
- Paprika Recipe Manager (www.paprikaapp.com): This app allows you to store recipes, meal plan, generate grocery lists, and more. (There is a charge for this app.)
- Eat Your Books (https://www.eatyourbooks.com/library/recipes?online-recipes=true): This app allows you to organize recipes from cookbooks that you own as well as from magazines, food blogs, and other sources. (There is a free version and a monthly charge version of this app.)

○ **Health Insurance**

- "Understanding Health Insurance Coverage" (www.thebalance.com/understanding-health-insurance-policy-2645652)
- "A Checklist for Adding a Baby to Health Insurance & Life Insurance" (https://budgeting.thenest.com/checklist-adding-baby-health-insurance-life-insurance-24159.html): This article by Amber Keefer is posted on the website thenest.com

CHAPTER EIGHT: FAMILY FINANCES AND SAFEGUARDS

○ **Budget Guidance and Worksheets:** Go to the following websites for guidance; search for personal or household budget information.
  - kiplinger.com (www.kiplinger.com)
  - Kiplinger Budget Worksheet (www.kiplinger.com/kiplinger-tools/spending/t007-s001-budgeting-worksheet-a-household-budget-for-today-a/index.php)

○ **Tax Records—How Long to Keep**
  - IRS website page (www.irs.gov/businesses/small-businesses-self-employed/how-long-should-i-keep-records)

○ **Estate Planning**
  - "Estate Planning Basics" (www.thebalance.com/estate-planning-4073957): You'll find information on essential documents, planning, templates, and more.

○ **Life Insurance**
  - "Life Insurance for New Parents" (www.policygenius.com/life-insurance/life-insurance-for-new-parents/#when-should-new-parents-buy-life-insurance): Article written for Policygenius by Logan Sachon and Rebecca Shoenthal, Published August 13, 2020.

RESOURCES BY CATEGORY
AND ADDITIONAL RESOURCES

You can find these and other resources on my website, karenbongiorno.com (www.karenbongiorno.com).

FAMILY HEALTH AND WELLNESS
○ **Healthy Living**
- **Children's Vaccination Schedules**—The CDC (Centers for Disease Control and Prevention) has the schedules shown below on their website. You can use their schedules to keep track of your child's vaccines.
  - "Immunizations and Developmental Milestones for Your Child from Birth through Six Years Old" (www.cdc.gov/vaccines/parents/downloads/mile stones-tracker.pdf): Use this chart to fill in the date of each immunization as well as your child's developmental milestones.
  - "Recommended Child and Adolescent Immunization Schedule for Ages Eighteen Years or Younger" (www.cdc.gov/vaccines/schedules/downloads/child/0-18yrs-child-combined-schedule.pdf): This chart

shows the immunizations your child will need from birth through the age of eighteen.

- "The Family Dinner Project" (https://thefamilydinner project.org): Eating dinner together regularly as a family benefits children's emotional health and well-being. The Family Dinner Project explains these benefits and gives ways to make dinner fun and engaging. It lists conversation starters by age and gives recipes and resources for involving your neighborhood, organizations, and your children's schools in community dinners to support healthy dinner habits.

- "Why Is Sleep Important?" (www.nhlbi.nih.gov/node/ 4605): This information from the National Heart, Lung, and Blood Institute (NHLBI) explains the importance of sleep on one's emotional and physical well-being as well as one's brain, body function, and safety.

- "National Sleep Foundation Recommends New Sleep Times" (www.sleephealthjournal.org/pb/assets/raw/ Health%20Advance/journals/sleh/NSF_press_release_ on_new_sleep_durations_2-2-15.pdf): This press release, published in *Sleep Health: The Journal of the National Sleep Foundation* (www.sleepfoundation.org), gives guidelines on how much sleep is needed at each age.

- "How Much Screen Time Is OK for My Kid(s)?" (www. commonsensemedia.org/screen-time/how-much-screen-time-is-ok-for-my-kids): Common Sense Media's website is an excellent resource for determining limits at every age. (When your children are older and begin to be exposed to and use social media, you'll want to be educated on potential problems and the downside of social media.)

○ **General Health Information**

- National Institute of Health (NIH) (www.nih.gov/health-information): The NIH is part of the US Department of Health and Human Services. It is the center for federal medical research and is one of the world's premier research centers. The NIH conducts its own research and supports research at universities, hospitals, and other medical research centers throughout the world. Their website has a wealth of information on healthy living, disease symptoms, and prevention as well as new research studies and findings.

- CDC (Centers for Disease Control and Prevention) (www.cdc.gov): The CDC is the health protection agency of the US Department of Health and Human Services. The site has credible information on health, well-being, vaccines, the diseases that each vaccine prevents, up-to-date scientific health information, resources, and more.

○ **Mom's Health Concerns**

- "Postpartum Depression—Topic Overview" (www.webmd.com/depression/guide/postpartum-depression#1): This article from the website WebMD gives a good description of postpartum depression.

- "Mommy Mentors Help Fight the Stigma of Postpartum Mood Disorder" (www.npr.org/sections/health-shots/2017/09/29/554280219/mommy-mentors-help-fight-the-stigma-of-postpartum-mood-disorder?utm_source=npr_newsletter&utm_medium=email&utm_content=20171001&utm_campaign=&utm_term=?utm_source=npr_newsletter&utm_

medium=email&utm_content=20171001&utm_
campaign=&utm_term=): This article comes from
National Public Radio's *Health News,* September 29,
2017. It explains how a Florida program connects
women to support one another through the emotional
difficulties of postpartum. It includes information for
connecting mothers who live outside of Florida who
want this same kind of support.

○ **Health Insurance**

- ▪ "Understanding Health Insurance Coverage" (www.the
balance.com/understanding-health-insurance-policy-
2645652#help-%20understandingyour-health-%20
insurance-policy-basics): This link to The Balance
website, thebalance.com, leads to an article by Mila
Araujo, updated October 31, 2019, that explains how
deductibles, co-payments, and basic health insurance
coverage work.
- ▪ "A Checklist for Adding a Baby to Health Insurance
& Life Insurance" (https://budgeting.thenest.com/
checklist-adding-baby-health-insurance-life-insurance-
24159.html): This blog article written by Amber Keefer
appears on The Nest website, thenest.com.

PARENT EDUCATION

There is much to learn as a parent. I believe this starts with
knowing and understanding your child. It's helpful to understand how your child's growth stages, temperament, and
abilities affect him or her. The websites shown below have
information on children's temperament, development, and
other concerns.

○ **Children's Temperament**
  ▪ "The Nine Temperament Traits" (https://child developmentinfo.com/child-development/temperament_ and_your_child/temp2/#.XL4-Cy_Mx-U)
○ **Children's Development**
  ▪ "Child Development Basics" (www.cdc.gov/ncbddd/ childdevelopment/facts.html): This website from the CDC public agency (Centers for Disease Control and Prevention) has information on children's developmental milestones, healthy development, positive parenting practices, research articles, and developmental screening and monitoring.
○ **Attention and Learning Concerns**
  ▪ Understood (www.understood.org/en) is an association designed to support parents of children with attention and learning issues. It has over four million members consisting of parents, teachers, and guardians. Members work to strengthen and support their local schools through community connection and involvement.

BUILDING COMMUNITY AND VOLUNTEERING

We need support as mothers. We can help build supportive communities by joining, participating, and volunteering in local activities, organizations, and schools. The resources here provide information on organizations for new mothers and school volunteer organizations for when your child goes to school.

○ **Mother's Organizations**: When you become a mom, you'll want to connect with other moms. The following websites can help you find local as well as online mothers' and parents' organizations. There is also a website on creating your own organization if you cannot find an appropriate one in your area.

- Baby Center (https://community.babycenter.com/ groups): This website has information on many different kinds of online communities for mothers. Groups include mothers trying to get pregnant, baby names, discussions about toddlers, tweens, family relationships, and more.
- Meetup for Moms (www.meetup.com/topics/mommy-me/): Use any of the following search topics to help you find mothers' groups:
  - Moms (www.meetup.com/topics/moms/)
  - Playdates (www.meetup.com/topics/playgroup/)
  - Parents (www.meetup.com/topics/parents/)
  - Toddlers (www.meetup.com/topics/toddler/)
  - Babies (www.meetup.com/topics/babies/)
  - Preschoolers (www.meetup.com/topics/preschoolers/)
  - Work at Home Moms (www.meetup.com/topics/wahm/)
  - Working Moms (www.meetup.com/topics/working moms/)
  - New Parents (www.meetup.com/topics/new-parents/)
  - Kids (www.meetup.com/topics/kids/)
  - Expecting Parents (www.meetup.com/topics/expecting-parents/)
  - Create Your Own Meetup Group (https://secure. meetup.com/create/)

○ **School Volunteering:** During the course of your child's school years, you'll have the opportunity to volunteer or be a part of the support systems at her schools. The links shown below give an overview of these organizations: their purpose, structure, and volunteer opportunities.

- National Parent Teacher Association (PTA) (www.pta. org): National association of over four million members consisting of parents, teachers, and guardians. Members work to strengthen and support their local schools through community connection and involvement.
- "What Every Parent Should Know about Their School Board" (www.greatschools.org/gk/articles/school-board-candidates/): This article from the website GreatSchools.org (www.greatschools.org) explains the importance of knowing the function and responsibilities of school boards.
- "Beyond Money: Benefits of an Education Foundation" (www.aasa.org/SchoolAdministratorArticle.aspx?id= 10776): This article written by Mark M. Havens for the School Superintendents Association (AASA) website discusses school foundations' functions and the value in connecting within communities to do more than fundraising.
- The Role of the School Site Council (www.greatschools. org/gk/articles/the-role-of-the-school-site-council/): This website has information on the benefits of school site councils and what types of volunteer opportunities they offer.

CHILDREN'S EDUCATION

○ **Preschool:** Preschools have varying ideas that are reflected in how they structure and orient their programs. Often their approach may combine several theories. The resources shown here provide information on these differing philosophies.

- "Preschool Philosophies, A to Z" (www.greatschools. org/gk/articles/preschool-philosophies/): This article from the website Great Schools.org details seven types of preschools and explanations on how each type implements its approach to child development and learning. (On the website, under the "Parenting" tab, select "Raising kids" and then "Early learning," then search for "preschool philosophies.")
- "Challenge Success: Do You Know?" (www.challengesuccess.org/resources/research/do-you-know/): Download the Preschool PDF from this link. It is a "Do You Know" article from Challenge Success that summarizes research on the effect of influences and activities on preschool-aged children's lives. A discussion of academic-based vs. play-based preschools is included in this summary.

○ **Kindergarten**
  - "What Do Kids Learn in Kindergarten" (www.k5learning. com/blog/what-kids-learn-kindergarten): This article from the K5 Learning Blog gives an overview of what children learn in kindergarten.
  - K5 Learning Worksheets (www.k5learning.com/free-preschool-kindergarten-worksheets): This site has free downloadable worksheets for many different activities, offered by K5 Learning.

MOTHERS' EMPLOYMENT AND CAREERS

There is no consensus on the effect, good or bad, of mothers being employed full-time, part-time, or taking care of their children full-time. I believe doing what works best for your family is the ideal way to make that choice. This choice can change over time as circumstances change. It is a tough decision for each family to find the balance that works. Workable solutions and resources are needed for mothers or parents during their child-raising years. Time off, flexible schedules, job sharing, childcare support, and more are useful accommodations that could benefit mothers or parents and companies as well. Building in alternatives that allow mothers or parents to continue their career paths would help retain experienced workers. The articles and books shown below discuss the challenges mothers/parents face in the workforce, potential solutions, and directions for change.

○ **Articles**

- "Two Jobs, Two New Parents: How to Negotiate Your New Reality," by Elissa Strauss, Parenting, *New York Times,* May 6, 2019.

- "If You Want Women to Move Up, You Have to Accommodate Mothers," by Rebecca Johnson, Opinion, *Wall Street Journal,* January 4, 2018. (www.wsj.com/articles/if-you-want-women-to-move-up-you-have-to-accommodate-mothers-1515110849)

- "Women Did Everything Right. Then Work Got 'Greedy,'" by Claire Cain Miller, *New York Times,* April 26, 2019.

- "The Open Secret of Anti-Mom Bias at Work," by Katherine Goldstein, *New York Times,* May 16, 2018.

- "Upshot Letter: Our Anti-Parenting Bias," by David Leonhardt, *New York Times,* April 3, 2015.

- "A Labor Market Punishing to Mothers," by David Leonhardt, *New York Times,* August 3, 2010.

○ **Books**

- *Forget "Having It All": How America Messed Up Motherhood—and How to Fix It,* by Amy Westervelt. New York, NY: Seal Press, 2018. (https://www.amywestervelt.com/about)

- *Making Motherhood Work: How Women Manage Careers and Caregiving,* by Caitlyn Collins. Princeton, NJ: Princeton University Press, 2019. (https://caitlyncollins.com)
- *Unfinished Business: Women, Men, Work, Family,* by Anne-Marie Slaughter. New York, NY: Random House, 2016. (https://scholar.princeton.edu/slaughter/home)
- *The Second Shift: Working Families and the Revolution at Home,* by Arlie R. Hochschild. New York, NY: Penguin Group, 2012. (https://sociology.berkeley.edu/professor-emeritus/arlie-r-hochschild)

MEDIA AND SOCIAL MEDIA GUIDELINES

Studies and articles continue to point out the drawbacks for children of too much exposure to social media. Guidelines for healthy limits of time spent on social media differ by age. You'll find guidelines for healthy limits in the research information and articles shown here.

○ **General Information**
  - "How Much Screen Time Is OK for My Kid(s)?" (www.commonsensemedia.org/screen-time/how-much-screen-time-is-ok-for-my-kids): Common Sense Media (www.commonsensemedia.org) is a nonprofit organization that is dedicated to understanding how technology and social media affect children and families. They provide resources for parents, educators, and advocates to educate them on the pros and cons of technology across the spectrum from social media, to games, apps, TV, movies, virtual reality, and more. You can find age-appropriate guidelines for screen content and limits for your children.
  - "Have Smartphones Destroyed a Generation?" (www.

theatlantic.com/magazine/archive/2017/09/has-
the-smartphone-destroyed-a-generation/534198/?utm_
source=eb): In this important article written for *The
Atlantic* magazine, author Jean M. Twenge, a professor of
psychology at San Diego State University and the author
of *Generation Me* and *iGen*, discusses the adverse effects
of smartphone use on children. She argues that children
are on the brink of a mental health crisis.

- American Academy of Pediatrics—Recommendations
  for Children's Media Use (https://healthychildren
  .org/English/news/Pages/AAP-Announces-New-
  Recommendations-for-Childrens-Media-Use.aspx):
  The AAP recommends that children under the age of
  two have minimal exposure to media. This website has
  research and guidelines for children's use of media and
  on the necessity of parents interacting with their children during media use.

- Wait Until 8th Pledge (https://www.waituntil8th.org):
  This website advocates for children waiting until eighth
  grade to get a smartphone. It provides background and
  resources to parents to assist them in gathering like-
  minded parents in their communities.

FAMILY FINANCES AND SAFEGUARDS

- **Budgeting: Budget Guidance and Worksheets:** Go to
  the following websites for guidance; search for personal
  or household budget information.
  - kiplinger.com (www.kiplinger.com)
  - Kiplinger Budget Worksheet (www.kiplinger.com/
    kiplinger-tools/spending/t007-s001-budgeting-work
    sheet-a-household-budget-for-today-a/index.php)

○ **Taxes: Tax Records—How Long to Keep**
  - IRS website page (www.irs.gov/businesses/small-businesses-self-employed/how-long-should-i-keep-records)
○ **Estate Planning—Wills and Living Trusts**
  - "Estate Planning Basics" (www.thebalance.com/estate-planning-4073957): You'll find information on essential documents, planning, templates, and more.
○ **Life Insurance for Parents**
  - "Life Insurance for New Parents" (www.policygenius.com/life-insurance/life-insurance-for-new-parents/#when-should-new-parents-buy-life-insurance): Article written for Policygenius by Logan Sachon and Rebecca Shoenthal, Published August 13, 2020.
○ **General Information**
  - Social Security Information (https://www.ssa.gov/myaccount/)

ORGANIZATION

○ **Calendars**
  - Calendar Apps—There are many calendar apps you can download to your smartphone to help you manage your family calendar. Below are two that I like.
    - Family Organizer by Sevenlogics (www.sevenlogics.com): This mobile app allows you to record and keep track of your to-dos, recipes, and more. (The free version has advertising.)
    - Iphone Week Cal (https://www.weekcal.com): I like the agenda view of this app for the iPhone.

- Paper Calendar
  - I like the Moleskine Weekly Planner: https://us.mole
    skine.com/planners/weekly-planners/0102-2
  - I plan to publish my own two-page weekly calendar
    for moms.
○ **Recipe Organizing:** I like to organize my recipes by category in a three-ring binder. I put each recipe in a clear page protector to shield them from spills. I also use Pinterest. Below are online sources for organizing your recipes.

- Pinterest My Recipes (www.pinterest.com/myrecipes/
  _created/): This site allows you to search, save, and organize recipes.
- Paprika Recipe Manager (https://www.paprikaapp.com): This app allows you to store recipes, meal plan, generate grocery lists, and more. (There is a charge for this app.)
- Eat Your Books (https://www.eatyourbooks.com/library/
  recipes?online-recipes=true): This app allows you to organize recipes from cookbooks that you own as well as from magazines, food blogs, and other sources. (There is a free version and a monthly charge version of this app.)

In Chapter Ten:

APPENDIX

◇◇◇◇◇◇◇◇◇◇◇◇◇◇◇◇◇◇

○ **TIPS AND SUGGESTIONS–BIRTH TO KINDERGARTEN**

○ **REFERENCE INFORMATION—BIRTH TO KINDERGARTEN**

○ **FAMILY ORGANIZATION TABLES**
  1. Family Health Care
  2. School and Activities
  3. Household and Auto—Service and
     Maintenance Providers
  4. Social, Entertaining, and Vacations
  5. Household Budget and Bill Paying
  6. Financial Accounts, Insurance Policies, and Taxes
  7. Safeguards: Estate Planning, Insurance,
     and Important Documents

○ **SAMPLE FAMILY BUDGET**

○ **TYPES OF REFERENCE INFORMATION TABLES**
  1. Quick Refrence Information
  2. Current-Term Reference Information
  3. Long-Term Reference Information

○ **USEFUL FORMS**
  ▪ Emergency Reference Form
  ▪ Health-Care Notes Form

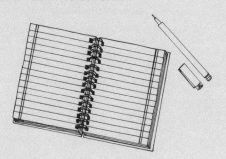

Chapter Ten

APPENDIX

TIPS AND SUGGESTIONS— BIRTH THROUGH KINDERGARTEN * Ongoing Based on the Age Shown	
YOUR CHILD'S WELL-BEING	✴ Put aside your phone and electronics when feeding your baby/child and during one-on-one time. ✴ Limit screen time for your child: common sensemedia.org is an excellent resource for determining limits at every age. ✴ Age 4–5 months: Read to your child and show her the pictures. ✴ Age 2+: Read with your child each day. Show her the letters and words sometimes, as she is interested, increasing as she gets older. ✴ Preschool and kindergarten: Schedule play-dates for your child with classmates. ✴ Age 2+: Jobs for your child: help put away books and toys.
YOUR WELL-BEING	✴ Realize you won't have direct control over your time and energy when you are with your child. Decide what your priorities are for the time you have; be reasonable with your expectations.

(continued on next page) ▶

▶ *(continued from previous page)*

YOUR WELL-BEING	✶ Set aside time each day, even if it is brief, to give yourself a break. Establish a meaningful ritual for this time. ✶ Arrange with your spouse, partner, or caregiver to care for your child at a regular time each week to give you time for personal restoration. Do something you enjoy (no tasks).
FAMILY	✶ Eat dinner together as a family. ✶ Get out with your spouse or partner regularly for date night. ✶ Kindergarten: Family vacation plans will need to coordinate with school breaks.
YOUR VILLAGE/ COMMUNITY	✶ Stay in touch with your mom friends from playgroup and other organizations. ✶ Socialize with your neighbors. Plan play-dates with neighboring families. ✶ Preschool and kindergarten: Volunteer at school if possible. ✶ Preschool and kindergarten: Get to know parents and children at your child's school. ✶ Kindergarten: Join the PTA or Parent Association; go to meetings. ✶ Kindergarten: Consider volunteering with the PTA/PA.
ACTIVITIES AND/OR AFTERCARE	✶ Preschool and kindergarten: Learn about children's after-school activities offered on or off campus through your school, town recreation department, or local individuals as soon as they are available (usually two months before the quarter begins). Enroll your child with a friend, if you can. Sign up ASAP, as spots fill quickly. ✶ Preschool and kindergarten: Sign your child up for aftercare, if needed.
SUMMER CAMPS/ ACTIVITIES	✶ Preschool and kindergarten: Look at options in January. Sign your child up with a friend (if possible).

(continued on next page) ▶

▶ *(continued from previous page)*

PRESCHOOL AND KINDERGARTEN	✱ Review take-home items with your child. ✱ Go to parent education and other parent meetings. ✱ Learn how school administrators communicate with parents. ✱ Look at school communications routinely to keep up-to-date. ✱ Kindergarten: Go to Back-to-School Night to meet your child's teacher. Find out how the teacher communicates with parents: e-mail, website, voice mail, etc.
PRIVATE SCHOOL	✱ Preschool and kindergarten: Research elementary schools if you are considering alternatives to the local public school.

REFERENCE INFORMATION—BIRTH THROUGH KINDERGARTEN

☆ SAVE LONG-TERM

⇨ ENTER INFORMATION IN PERSONAL CALENDAR

❖ SAVE FOR THE CURRENT PERIOD

☆ **CHILD'S IMMUNIZATION RECORDS**
Keep track of your child's immunizations. Go to: www.cdc.gov/vaccines/parents/downloads/milestones-tracker.pdf for a printable immunization schedule.

☆ **CHILD'S HEALTH RECORDS—NOTES**
Keep the notes you take at pediatrician and other health-care appointments.

☆ **IMPORTANT CONTACTS REFERENCE LIST**
Keep your contact list updated and posted in your home for babysitters and other caregivers: include doctors, caregivers, hospital, emergency phone numbers, relatives, neighbors.

☆ **MEMBERSHIP DIRECTORY FOR YOUR COMMUNITY GROUP(S)** (if any)

(continued on next page) ▶

▶ *(continued from previous page)*

ACTIVITIES

❖ **Activity(s) Coach/ Instructor(s)' Name and Contact Info**

❖ **Website(s) Access Info**—if applicable

⇨ **Activity Schedule:** Enter all dates in your personal calendar.

⇨ **Car Pool Schedule** (if any): Enter all dates in your personal calendar.

☆ **Activity Roster(s)**
- Children's and parents' names
- Addresses
- Phone numbers, e-mail addresses

PRESCHOOL

❖ **Preschool Contact Info and Web Access Info**— if applicable.

⇨ **School Calendar**
- Enter important dates into your calendar.

☆ **Preschool Class Roster**
- Children's and parents' names
- Addresses
- Phone numbers, e-mail addresses

⇨ **School Calendar for Next Year**
- Obtain when available for planning purposes; enter all dates in your personal calendar.

KINDERGARTEN

❖ **School Administration Contact Info and Web Access Info**

⇨ **School Calendar:** Enter important dates in your personal calendar. You may be able to download and sync the school calendar with your online calendar (if available at your school).

☆ **Kindergarten Class Roster**
- Children's and parents' names
- Addresses
- Phone numbers, e-mail addresses

⇨ **School Calendar for Next Year** Obtain when available for planning purposes; enter all dates in your personal calendar.

☆ **School Directory**

FAMILY REFERENCE INFORMATION—TABLE ONE
FAMILY HEALTH CARE AND INSURANCE—PROVIDERS, HEALTH AND PRESCRIPTIONS RECORDS

Types of Reference Information to Save

○ **Quick-Reference Information** should be saved where it can be accessed quickly and easily in your Smartphone Contacts app, Notes app, Calendar, or as a separate physical or online summary document.

○ **Current-Term Reference Information** is information you'll need occasionally during the current period.

○ **Long-Term Reference Information** should be saved indefinitely for reference.

Create separate Health-Care Records files for each family member to save with information such as immunization records, your notes from health-care appointments, research, and prescriptions information. You can create files online or use physical notebooks and/or files to store this information.

HEALTH-CARE PROVIDERS	CONTACT INFO, WEBSITES, AND APPS
○ **Doctors** ■ Pediatrician, Pediatric Nurse(s), Office Manager ■ Pediatric Dentist ■ OB/GYN ■ Family Primary Care Doctor ■ Dentist ■ Other Doctors ■ Names of Assistants, Nurses, Office Managers ○ **Pharmacy** ○ **Prescription Service** ○ **After Hours Emergency Care Facility**	**Quick Reference Info** ○ **Doctor, Dentist, Pharmacy, After Hours/Urgent Care, Hospital, Insurance Company Providers:** ■ Business Phone Numbers ■ After Hours Phone Numbers ■ E-mail Addresses ■ Street Addresses ■ Emergency Reference Guide (See the Emergency Reference Guide form in the Appendix. Create your

(continued on next page) ▶

▶ *(continued from previous page)*

○ **Hospital**

○ **Poison Control Phone Numbers**

MEDICAL/DENTAL INSURANCE PROVIDERS

Quick Reference Info

- Name of Insurance Company
- Main Insurance Plan Identification Number(s)
- Family Members' ID numbers

○ **Contact Info**
- Business Phone Numbers
- E-mail Addresses

○ **Providers' Websites and Apps**

Most insurance companies have websites and apps with online access for their customers. These allow you to review your insurance claims, billing, reimbursement information, and more, using a user ID and password.

- Bookmark provider websites.
- Bookmark portal websites.
- Download all available provider apps.

own guide by filling in your providers' information as shown.) Post this Guide in your home for babysitters and other caregivers.

○ **Providers' Websites and Apps**
Most doctors, health practices, and hospitals offer patient portal websites or apps that allow you to access your health records, send notes to your doctor, and schedule appointments, using a secure login.

- Bookmark provider websites.
- Bookmark patient portal websites.
- Download all available provider apps.
- Save User IDs and login passwords for websites and apps

MEDICAL/DENTAL INSURANCE COVERAGE INFORMATION

Current-Term Reference Info

It's important to know your insurance coverage terms: what your insurance covers, the cost, your deductible and co-pay amounts, and more. You should be able to find this information by logging into

(continued on next page) ▶

▶ *(continued from previous page)*

- Save user IDs and login passwords for websites and apps.

○ **Medical and Dental Insurance Cards**
Bring these cards to health-care visits. They show the insurance plan and family member ID numbers, as well as the insurance company contact information.

your insurance company website. (Note 1)

Open enrollment for health insurance happens annually, usually in November. This is the time to review insurance options for your family.

Of course, when your new baby arrives, you'll want to be sure to add her to your health insurance right away. (Note 2)

Notes

1. For more information on Health Insurance coverage, see: Understanding Your Health Insurance Policy on thebalance. com. www.thebalance.com/ understanding-health-insurance-policy-2645652#help-%20 understandingyour-health-%20 insurance-policy-basics)

2. Adding your baby to your health insurance plan: Call your insurance company to add coverage for your baby. Some insurance companies will want a social security number and a copy of the baby's birth certificate. See: Checklist for Adding a Baby to Health Insurance on the budgeting. thenest.com website (https:// budgeting.thenest.com/checklist-adding-baby-health-insurance-life-insurance-24159.html)

(continued on next page) ▶

▶ *(continued from previous page)*

HEALTH RECORDS

Current and Long-Term Reference Info

○ **IMMUNIZATION RECORDS**
For a printable immunization schedule, go to: www.cdc.gov/vaccines/parents/downloads/milestones-tracker.pdf

○ **NOTES**
(See Appendix for Health-Care Visit Notes form.)
Save notes (as needed) from appointments and conversations with doctors, dentists, specialists, etc.

○ **RESEARCH INFO**
Keep information you've collected or gathered through research for relevant health or medical conditions.

PRESCRIPTIONS*	PRESCRIPTIONS RENEWALS	PRESCRIPTIONS HISTORY
Current-Term Reference Information	Enter the following in your Personal Calendar:	**Long-Term Reference Information**
▪ Medication Name	▪ Enter all prescription renewal dates in your calendar.	▪ Medication Name
▪ Medication Dosage		▪ Medication Dosage
▪ Prescription #	▪ Schedule a follow-up doctor appointment if a renewal prescription is needed.*	▪ Dates Taken
▪ Pharmacy and Address		▪ Notes—reason for taking
▪ Prescribing Doctor		
▪ Instructions and Precautions		
▪ Refills (if applicable)	* Schedule the follow-appointment before you leave the doctor's office, if possible, or ask for a reminder notice. If neither of these is possible, then set a reminder in your calendar to book the follow-up appointment.	
▪ When to Renew (if applicable)		
* Most of this information will be on the prescription label or related material that you get from the pharmacy.		

FAMILY REFERENCE INFORMATION—TABLE TWO
HOUSEHOLD AND AUTO—SERVICE MAINTENANCE PROVIDERS

Types of Reference Information to Save

O **Quick Reference Information** should be saved where it can be accessed quickly and easily in your smartphone Contacts app, Notes app, Calendar, or as a separate physical or online summary document.

O **Current-Term Reference Information** is information you'll need occasionally during the current period.

O **Long-Term Reference Information** should be saved indefinitely for reference.

SERVICES AND MAINTENANCE PROVIDERS (as applicable)

O **Utilities**
  - Gas
  - Electric
  - Water
  - Phone - Landline
  - Phone - Mobile/Cell
  - Trash Service
  - Cable
  - Wi-fi
O **Subscriptions**
  - Digital and Print
  - Newspapers
  - Magazines
O **Entertainment Accounts**
  - Streaming Services
  - Others
O **Loyalty Rewards Programs**
  - Airlines
  - Retail
  - Other
O **Repesentative/Landlord for Rental Home or Apartment**

CONTACT INFO, WEBSITES, AND APPS FOR PROVIDERS

Quick Reference Info

Save the following for each provider (as needed):
  O Account Name/Number
  O Account Representative
  O Phone Numbers
  O E-mail Address
  O Street/Mailing Address
  O Download available apps.
  O Bookmark websites.
  O Websites and Apps Access Info; User IDs and Login Passwords

OTHER IMPORTANT NUMBERS

Quick Reference Info

Create a list of the numbers shown below:
  O Social Security Numbers (for each family member)
  O Drivers' License Numbers (for each family member)
  O Car(s) License Plate Number(s)

(continued on next page) ▶

▶ *(continued from previous page)*

○ **Home Repair and Appliance Services**

○ **House Cleaning Services**

○ **Auto Service**

AUTO RECORDS	RENTAL HOME OR APARTMENT RECORDS
Current-Term Reference Info	**Current-Term Reference Info**
○ Lease or Finance Records	○ Rental Documents
Long-Term Reference Info	
○ Service Records	
○ Title (Pink Slip) if owned—Keep original title(s) in safe deposit box or other secure location	

OWNED HOME RECORDS

Quick Reference Info	**Current-Term Reference Info**
○ Note the real estate tax due dates in your personal calendar. Example: April 10 and December 10	○ Semiannual real estate tax bills: Keep these where you can access them easily.
○ Make a note in your calendar or schedule a reminder ten days prior to the due dates for your semiannual real estate taxes to avoid a late payment penalty. Example: April 1 and December 1	**Long-Term Reference Info**
	○ Mortgage loan documents
	○ Appraisal (if you have one)
	○ Real estate improvements and substantial repair cost records
	○ Title to home, if you have no mortgage—Keep original title in safe deposit box or other secure location.

FAMILY REFERENCE INFORMATION—TABLE THREE
SCHOOL AND ACTIVITIES

Types of Reference Information to Save

○ **Quick Reference Information** should be saved where it can be accessed quickly and easily in your smartphone Contact app, Notes app, Calendar, or as a separate physical or online summary document.

○ **Current-Term Reference Information** is information you'll need occasionally during the current period.

○ **Long-Term Reference Information** should be saved indefinitely for reference.

SCHOOL ADMINISTRATION:
CONTACT INFO AND WEBSITES

Store often-needed school information in your smartphone for:
○ School Attendance Phone Line
○ School Office
○ Bookmark websites.
○ Save website user IDs and login passwords.

SCHOOL DIRECTORY*	SCHOOL CALENDARS(S)
Current-Term Reference Info	**Personal Calendar Info**
Be sure to purchase/obtain the school directory. (Usually you will receive a directory when you pay for membership in the PTA.) It's helpful to keep an extra copy of the directory in your car. The directory includes:	You may be able to download and/or sync the school calendar with your personal online calendar (if your school makes it available). If not, enter the school calendar dates shown below into your
○ **Contact Info for:**	**Personal Calendar:**
■ Administration and Teachers	○ Holidays
■ PTA	○ Teacher days
■ Foundation (if applicable)	○ Minimum days
■ Students and Parents	

(continued on next page) ▶

▶ *(continued from previous page)*

- Other information
  - School Calendar
  - Bell Schedule for Classes
  - Other

* Save the directory at the end of the school year for Long-Term Reference.

- Altered-schedule days
- Beginning and ending grading period dates
- Exam schedule dates (if applicable)

SCHOOL TEACHERS: CONTACT INFO AND WEBSITES

Quick Reference Info

Include the following information in contact info for each teacher:

- Teacher's Name
- Notes: Include preferred method of contact.
- Phone Number
- E-mail Address
- Bookmark websites.
- Save user IDs and login passwords.

SCHOOL CLASS INFO

Current-Term Reference Info

- Class Curriculum
- Class Guidelines
- Class Info and Teacher Handouts
- Schedule of Classes (beginning in middle school, when children have more than one teacher)
- School Directory*
- Class Roster*

* Save the School Directory and Class Roster at the end of the school year for Long-Term Reference.

ACTIVITIES: CONTACT INFO AND WEBSITES

Quick Reference Info

Include the following information in contact info for each activity:

- Activity Name
- Address
- Phone Number
- E-mail Address
- Coach/Teacher Name

ACTIVITY SCHEDULE

Personal Calendar

- Schedule - Input all schedule information

ACTIVITY INFORMATION

Current-Term Reference Info

- Rules for Class or Team

ACTIVITY CAR POOL

(if applicable)

Quick Reference Info

- Car Pool Participants
- Home Addresses
- Phone Numbers
- E-mail Addresses

▶ (continued from previous page)

O Notes: Include preferred method of contact
O Bookmark websites.
O Save user IDs and login passwords.

O Requirements for Parent Participatiion or Volunteer Opportunities

ACTIVITY ROSTER*

Current-Term Reference Info

Bring the roster to games, performances, practices, etc. If one is not available, you can make and distribute it to parents. Include:

O children's names and their parents' names
O home addresses and phone numbers
O children's corresponding uniform number, position, part, etc.

* After the activity ends, save the roster for Long-Term reference.

CAR POOL SCHEDULES

Personal Calendar

O Input days and times assigned for each driver.
O Note any guidelines you have agreed upon, such as providing snacks or assisting with changing clothes, shoes, etc.

FAMILY REFERENCE INFORMATION—TABLE FOUR
SOCIAL LISTS, ENTERTAINING, AND VACATIONS NOTES

Reference Information to Save

Create files online or use physical notebooks to save lists and notes. At the end of each year, add the current-year lists to the online folder or binder to save for Long-Term reference.

SOCIAL LISTS	VACATIONS AND ENTERTAINING NOTES
Quick Reference Info	**Long-Term Reference**

○ **Month-By-Month Dates to Remember** Create a Quick Reference Document for yearly occasions to remember.
 	
List by:
■ Date
■ Occasion
  - Birthday
  - Anniversary
  - Holiday
  - Other
 	
Current-Term Reference Info
 	
○ **Current-Year Gifts List**
  Include:
■ Date
■ Gift recipient name
■ Gift description
■ Occasion
	○ **Vacations**
	  Include:
	■ Dates
	■ Location(s)
	■ Who went
	■ Notes on memorable moments and highlights
	○ **Entertaining Notes—(Hosted at home or away)**
	Make brief notes about each occasion. Include:
	■ A copy of the online invitation or physical invitation (if you sent one)
	■ The occasion (dinner with friends, birthday celebration, holiday), date, time, and place
	■ Guests' names
	■ Menu—list each course as applicable:
	  - Drinks before, during, and after meal
	  - Appetizers
	  - Soup or salad
	  - Main course
	  - Dessert
	■ **Preparation Notes**—List the steps that can be done ahead of time and when to do them.
	■ **Decor Notes**—flowers, decorations, or theme for your gathering
	■ **Post-event notes**—brief highlights

(continued on next page) ▶

▶ *(continued from previous page)*

○ **Current-Year Holiday Card Recipients List**
Create a group within your Contacts app or make a reference document. Include:
- Names
- Addresses
- Notes (if any)

For Events Hosted at Home
Include:
- Serving dishes and place settings—flatware, plates, bowls, glasses, etc.
- Recipes—Note where to find each.
- Grocery list of ingredients to buy
- Catered or prepared foods (if applicable). Note where and when to pick up.

○ **House Guest Notes**
Make brief notes about your guests' visit. Include:
- Guests' names
- Dates of visit
- Notes on outings and activities

FAMILY REFERENCE INFORMATION—TABLE FIVE

HOUSEHOLD BUDGET AND BILL PAYING

Budget Guidelines

Determine your household budget by adding all monthly income and subtracting your expected monthly expenses. (*See: Sample Monthly Budget*, on page 189 or on page 245.) Remember to plan for annual expenses. Save funds each month by setting up automatic transfers of money from your checking account to your savings or investment accounts.

You can find additional financial guidance and a worksheet in the website below:

○ **kiplinger.com**
○ **Household Budget Worksheet** (www.kiplinger.com/kiplinger-tools/spending/t007-s001-budgeting-worksheet-a-household-budget-for-today-a/index.php)

(continued on next page) ▶

▶ *(continued from previous page)*

HOUSEHOLD BUDGET

Save your budget as a Quick Reference Document to refer to each month when paying your bills. Store it in the Notes app of your smartphone or, if you use a paper calendar, by placing a physical copy in there.

○ **Monthly Income**
  ▪ Sources

○ **Monthly Expenses**
  ▪ Mortgage or rent payment
  ▪ Groceries, personal and household care products
  ▪ Gas
  ▪ Auto payment(s)
  ▪ Student loans
  ▪ Utilities
  ▪ Activity costs
  ▪ Monthly membership fees
  ▪ Subscriptions
  ▪ Housecleaning and garden maintenance
  ▪ Entertainment
  ▪ Clothing
  ▪ Gifts
  ▪ Other

○ **Monthly Savings**
  ▪ Arrange monthly automatic transfers from your checking account for the amount you want to save each month.

BILL PAYING

Pay your bills on time by using one or more of the following Routine Payment Methods:

❖ **Automatic Payments:**
  ▪ Arrange monthly automatic debits from your checking account for bill payments.

  ▪ Arrange monthly automatic charges to your credit card for bill payments. (Pay off these monthly credit card charges each month to avoid interest charges.)

❖ Schedule specific bill payments on the same day each month. Example: on the 15th and 30th of the month

❖ Pay all other bills as soon as you receive them by mail or e-mail. (This way you deal with these bills just once.)

❖ Note bill payment due dates on your calendar with reminder notices. (Use this method if you do not use automatic or scheduled payments.)

FAMILY REFERENCE INFORMATION—TABLE SIX
FINANCIAL ACCOUNTS, INSURANCE POLICIES, AND TAXES

Types of Reference Information to Save

O **Quick Reference Information** should be saved where it can be accessed quickly and easily in your smartphone Contacts app, Notes app, Calendar, or as a separate physical or online summary document.

O **Current-Term Reference Information** is information you'll need occasionally during the current period.*

O **Long-Term Reference Information** should be saved indefinitely for reference.*

* Create files online or use physical notebooks and/or files to store this information.

FINANCIAL ACCOUNTS	FINANCIAL ACCOUNTS: CONTACT INFO, WEBSITES, AND APPS

O **Assets**
  ▪ Checking Accounts (See Records, Note 1)
  ▪ Savings Accounts
  ▪ Investment Accounts
 	
O **Liabilities**
  ▪ Credit Cards (Note 1)
  ▪ Loans (Note 2)
  ▪ Home Mortgage (Note 2)
  ▪ Auto Loans/Leases (Note 2)
  ▪ Lines of Credit (Note 2)
	Quick Reference Info
	
	Save the following for your financial accounts company providers:
	  ▪ Account Representative
	  ▪ Phone Numbers
	  ▪ Account Name
	  ▪ Account Number
	  ▪ Account Type
	  ▪ Download available apps.
	  ▪ Bookmark website.
	  ▪ Websites and Apps Access Info; User IDs and Login Passwords
	  ▪ E-mail Address
	  ▪ Street/Mailing Address

(continued on next page) ▶

▶ *(continued from previous page)*

Notes

1. Create a list of automatic monthly charges to your checking accounts and credit cards (if any), e.g., health club fees, utilities, subscriptions. Save this list for <u>Current-term reference</u>. Be sure to update automatic payment accounts when you receive axnew or replacement card.

2. Keep a copy of loan documents or create a Summary Document for each loan with the following information:

- Loan Amount
- Loan Origination Date
- Loan Interest Rate
- Loan Due Date
- Monthly Payment Date
- Monthly Payment Amount

Save this information for <u>Current-term Reference</u>.

INSURANCE POLICY ACCOUNTS	INSURANCE ACCOUNTS: CONTACT INFO, WEBSITES, AND APPS	INSURANCE RECORDS
○ **Life Insurance** (Note 3) ○ **Auto Insurance** (Note 4) ○ **Home or Renter's Insurance** ○ **Other Insurance** ○ **Umbrella Policy** ○ **Flood Insurance** ○ **Earthquake Insurance** ○ **Home or Renter's Insurance** ○ **Additional Riders** (Note 5)	**Quick Reference Info** Save the following: • Agent Representative • Phone Numbers • E-mail Address • Street/Mailing Address (if needed) • Download available apps	**Current-Term Reference Info** Save or know how to access the following information online: ○ Declarations Page for each insurance policy. This shows:

(continued on next page) ▶

▶ *(continued from previous page)*

Notes—(cont.)

3. Life Insurance: You and your spouse/partner may want to increase your life insurance before or soon after your baby is born. (See Table Seven for further discussion of life insurance.)

4. Auto Insurance: You'll need to bring a copy of your auto insurance declaration page when you volunteer to drive for a school trip.

5. Extra insurance riders insure your extra-valuable property such as jewelry, antiques, electronics, etc. Save your purchase receipts/documentation and/or appraisals for these to provide evidence of their value.

- Bookmark website.
- Website and App Access Info; User IDs and Login Passwords

- Type of Policy (home, auto, life, etc.)
- Policy Number
- Policy Term—dates the policy is in effect
- Insurance Amount
- Premium cost of insurance policy
- Deductible—the amount you pay before you receive reimbursement from the insurance company when you report a loss

(continued on next page) ▶

▶ *(continued from previous page)*

TAX SERVICES— CONTACT INFO, WEBSITES, AND APPS

Quick Reference Info

O **Tax Accountant**
O **Bookkeeper**
O **Other**

Extra Save the following for the above tax service providers:

- Phone Numbers
- E-mail Address
- Street/Mailing Address
- Download available apps (if applicable)
- Bookmark websites (if applicable)
- Save websites and apps access info, user IDs and login passwords (if applicable)

TAX RECORDS*

Current and Long-Term Reference Info

Current-Term Reference Records
Save all tax-related receipts and documents that you accumulate throughout the year in a current-year tax collection file. These will be needed to prepare your annual tax returns.

- Receipts/records for deductible purchases or charitable donations
- Income and expense records for personal business, partnerships, etc.
- Year-end financial and investment account statements
- W-2(s)
- Tax statements from financial investments, insurance, real estate taxes, mortgage interest, etc.

Long-Term Reference Records
Save the following:

- Annual State Tax Returns
- Annual Federal Tax Returns

* To find out how long you need to keep tax-related records, go to the IRS website page: "How Long Should I Keep Records?" (www.irs.gov/businesses/small-businesses-self-employed/how-long-should-i-keep-records)

FAMILY REFERENCE INFORMATION—TABLE SEVEN
SAFEGUARDS: ESTATE PLANNING,
INSURANCE, AND IMPORTANT DOCUMENTS

<u>Types of Reference Information to Save</u>

○ **Quick Reference Information** should be saved where it can be accessed quickly and easily in your smartphone Contacts app, Notes app, Calendar, or as a separate physical or online summary document.
○ **Current-Term Reference Information** is information you'll need occasionally during the current period.*
○ **Long-Term Reference Information** should be saved indefinitely for reference.*

* Create files online or use physical notebooks and/or files to store this information.

ESTATE PLANNING INFORMATION AND INSURANCE

A simple will and living trust will protect and provide for your minor child or children in the unlikely event that you or your spouse dies prematurely or both of you die prematurely. You can find more information on estate planning at the website thebalance.com (https://www.thebalance.com/estate-planning-4073957). Review the information under Estate Planning Basics.

WILL*

The most important reason for having a will is that it names the guardian(s) you have chosen to raise your minor child or children. It also states how your assets will be distributed when you die.

REVOCABLE (LIVING) TRUST AGREEMENT*

The benefit of having a trust is that it allows your child or children to avoid the lengthy probate process that would occur without having it in place. It also keeps information about the assets and their distribution private.

* Keep the originals in your safe deposit box or other secure location. Be sure a trusted family member or an advisor knows where to locate these. Keep a copy of each document at home for Current-Term Reference.

(continued on next page) ▶

▶ *(continued from previous page)*

LIFE INSURANCE

Term life insurance is an effective and simple way to provide for your minor child. You and your spouse should name one another as beneficiary. If you want to name your child as your beneficiary, you will need to open a custodial account under the UTMA or UGMA law (depending on your state residency) to do so. See the website Policygenius.com (www.policygenius.com/life-insurance/life-insurance-for-new-parents/#when-should-new-parents-buy-life-insurance) to find answers to the questions new parents have about buying insurance.

ESTATE PLANNING & INSURANCE CONTACT INFO, WEBSITES, AND APPS

- ○ **Children's Guardian(s)**
- ○ **Executor(s) for Will**
- ○ **Attorney Who Drafted Will**
- ○ **Attorney Who Drafted Trust**
- ○ **Trustees for Trust—** (if applicable)
- ○ **Insurance Policy Representative**

Quick Reference Info

Save the following for the individuals shown above:

- ○ Phone Numbers
- ○ E-mail Addresses
- ○ Home and Business Addresses
- ○ Bookmark websites.
- ○ Website Access Info; User IDs and Password
- ○ Website Portal(s) Access Info; User IDs and Login Passwords (if applicable)

ADDITIONAL ORIGINAL LEGAL DOCUMENTS*

Current-Term Reference Info

Make copies of the following:

- ○ **Birth Certificates**
- ○ **Adoption Decree** (if applicable)
- ○ **Marriage Certificate**
- ○ **Passports**
- ○ **Social Security Cards** (if available)
- ○ **Title to Home** (if no mortgage)
- ○ **Title to Auto** (if no loan)

* Keep originals in your safe deposit box or other secure location.

SAMPLE MONTHLY BUDGET
For a Family with a Net Income of $4000 Each Month

Semimonthly Net Income Received on 15th of each Month = $2000		Semimonthly Net Income Received on 30th of each Month = $2000	
Monthly Expenses/Bills:	**Bills to Pay on the 15th**	**Monthly Expenses/Bills:**	**Bills to Pay on the 30th**
▪ Utilities (1)	$200	▪ Mortgage/ Rent Payment	$1,500
▪ Monthly Cash/ Entertainment (2)	$300	▪ Auto Payment(s)	$300
▪ Food, Sundries, Gas (3)	$500	▪ Household Expenses (4)	$200
▪ Student/Other Loans/ Credit Cards	$200	**Total Expenses to Pay on the 30th**	**$2,000**
Total Expenses to Pay on the 15th	**$1,200**		
Savings	$800	Savings	$0

Monthly Savings = $800	Annual Savings = $9,600
Save $400 Monthly for Yearly Expenses (5)	**$4,800—Yearly Expenses $400 x 12 = $4,800 (5)**
Save $400 Monthly for Long-Term Goals (6)	**$4,800—Long-Term Goals $400 x 12 = $4,800 (6)**

Notes

(1) Utility Costs: These costs will vary from month to month. Set an average amount in your budget. If utilities cost less than the set amount in one month, then roll the extra amount to the next month. If in another month, utilities cost more than the set amount, use money rolled from prior months to cover that month's higher cost. Adjust the average set amount as needed.

(2) Monthly Cash/Entertainment: It's easy to lose track of cash and entertainment spending. This is an important category to monitor.

(3) Food, Sundries, and Gas: These costs will vary (similar to utility costs). Set an average amount in your budget to manage your spending and adjust as necessary.

(continued on next page) ▶

▶ *(continued from previous page)*

(4) Household Expenses: Repairs, maintenance, etc. will vary from month to month. Again, set an average amount in your budget and adjust as needed.

(5) Yearly Expense Savings: Use these savings to cover your large expenses that aren't monthly recurring costs. Large expenses include insurance premiums, vacation, real estate taxes (if applicable), big purchases or expenses such as home projects, furniture, and more.

(6) Savings for Long-Term Goals: These are annual savings that you will add to each year to fund your long-term goals such as a down payment for a home, college savings account(s), retirement account(s), etc.

☆ TYPES OF FAMILY REFERENCE INFORMATION TABLE

Chapter Seven, *Family Organization*, introduced types of information. The table below summarizes these types: Quick Reference Information, Current-Term Reference Information, and Long-Term Reference Information.

TYPES OF FAMILY REFERENCE INFORMATION

Quick Reference Information

This is frequently needed information that is stored for fast retrieval.

WHAT TO STORE FOR QUICK REFERENCE	WHERE TO STORE QUICK REFERENCE INFO
❖ **Contacts** Store all contacts in the Contacts app: Include any websites and websites' access information, i.e., user IDs and passwords. Bookmark websites and download apps for easy retrieval. ▪ Family ▪ Personal Friends ▪ Doctors ▪ FamilyHealth Insurance— include each family member's insurance ID number ▪ Organizations ▪ School Administration ▪ Teachers ▪ Businesses ▪ Financial Contacts and Account Numbers ▪ Insurance: Home, Car, etc. ▪ Home Maintenance Services ▪ Utilities ▪ Parents of Your Child's Friends ▪ Car Pool Drivers	❖ **Personal Calendar** Enter: ▪ All current schedules ▪ Appointments ▪ Important dates ❖ **Smartphone—** Your smartphone is an excellent way to store Quick Reference Information because you will almost always have your phone with you. ▪ Contacts app: The Contacts app can hold all your contacts plus additional information. Example: Add your family members' individual insurance ID numbers to the contact information you have for health insurance. ▪ Notes app: Use the Notes app to store Quick Reference Information Documents. Example: Month-by-month list of dates to remember. Lock notes that have sensitive information.

(continued on next page) ▶

▶ *(continued from previous page)*

- Activity Teachers/ Instructors and Coaches

❖ **Quick Reference Information Documents—** Create Quick Reference Information Documents that summarize information you need regularly. (I realized I was constantly looking up or searching for the same information, so I began to store it in a way that allowed me to access it quickly.)
  - Class Roster
  - Current Year/Season Rosters—include:
    - Children's Names
    - Parents' Names
    - Uniform #'s or Part Description, e.g. Dorothy in *The Wizard of Oz*
  - Frequently Used Information
    - Monthly Budget
    - Month-by-Month Dates to Remember
  - Important Numbers
    - Social Security Numbers
    - Drivers' License Numbers
    - Car License Numbers

- Photo app: Take photos of Quick Reference Information Documents that have lists and summaries of information you use regularly. Store these in photo folders for fast retrieval.
- Cloud Service—Upload Quick Reference Information Documents to the cloud to access from anywhere.

❖ **Physical Calendar** (if you use a physical/paper calendar)—You can store physical copies of your Quick Reference Information Documents in your calendar.

(continued on next page) ▶

▶ *(continued from previous page)*

Current-Term Reference Information

This is information that is needed occasionally during the current period. An example of information to save for current-term reference is a list of team practice guidelines your child's coach hands out to parents. It's nice to have a copy of it during the current season, but you can discard it after the season ends.

At the end of the year, go through your current-term information to throw out anything you no longer need.

Some current-term information will become long-term reference information after the current period, semester, season, or year ends. Archived mail is a good example of current information that can be moved to long-term reference.

WHAT TO STORE FOR CURRENT-TERM REFERENCE

❖ **Family Health Info***
  ■ Immunization Schedule
  ■ Notes You've Made from Doctors/Other Care Providers
  ■ Research Information (if any)

❖ **Guidelines, Notes, Volunteer Requirements for:**
  ■ Teams
  ■ Activities
  ■ Organizations
  ■ Classrooms

❖ **Financial Info**
  ■ Home Mortgage Terms: Apartment or Home Rental Agreement*
  ■ Current Year: Tax Collection File Items

WHERE TO STORE CURRENT-TERM REFERENCE INFO

Use any of the methods shown here or a combination for storing your current-term reference information.

❖ **Physical Files and Notebooks**
Files: Use a separate file for each category of information, e.g., Finance, Health, Activity, etc.
Notebooks: Use a notebook for a single large category, e.g., one notebook for Family Health, with separate tabs for each family member.

❖ **Computer Files, Folders, and Scans**
  ■ Files: File information online in labeled files.

(continued on next page) ▶

▶ *(continued from previous page)*

- Insurance Declaration Pages

❖ **Copies of Important Documents and Related Info**
  - Copy of Original Will and Location
  - Copy of Living Trust Agreement and Location
  - Names of Guardians and Contact Info
  - Attorney Who Drafted Will and Living Trust and Contact Info
  - Marriage Certificate
  - Birth Certificate(s)
  - Adoption Decrees (if applicable)
  - Copy of Passports Information Pages
  - Other Original Legal Agreements (if any)

* Keep, also, for Long-Term Reference. See Below.

- Folders: Use folders to group files into categories online.
- Scans: Scan info into a PDF to save online in designated files and folders.

❖ **Online Mailbox Files and Folders***
Online mailbox files and folders can be archived.
  - Files: Set up and label mailbox files to save e-mails for reference.
  - Folders: Set up and label mailbox folders to save e-mail files by category.

❖ **Physical Directories***
  - School
  - Organizations

* Keep, also, for Long-Term Reference. See Below.

Long-Term Reference Information

This is information to save indefinitely for reference.

WHAT TO STORE FOR LONG-TERM REFERENCE	WHERE TO STORE LONG-TERM REFERENCE INFO
❖ **Health Records**	❖ **Physical Files and Notebooks**
❖ **Financial Records**	
❖ **Insurance Records**	❖ **Computer Files, Folders, Scans**
❖ **Home Improvement Records**	
❖ **Directories, Rosters**	❖ **Online Mailbox Files and Folders**

(continued on next page) ▶

▶ *(continued from previous page)*

❖ **Valuable Original Documents**
Store documents in a safe deposit box.
  - Marriage Certificate
  - Birth Certificates
  - Adoption Decrees (if applicable)
  - Passports
  - Social Security Cards
  - Title to Home (if no mortgage)
  - Title to Auto(s) (if no loan)

❖ **Physical Calendars**
Store with prior year calendars.

❖ **Physical Collections, e.g., Artwork**

❖ **Social Notes and Lists Collections**
Store in file folders or notebooks.
  - Prior Years, Month-by-Month Dates to Remember
  - Annual Lists of Holiday Card Recipients
  - Prior Years, Annual Lists of Gifts Given
  - Entertaining Notes
  - Vacation and Travel Notes
  - Guest Notes

❖ **Directories and Rosters**
Store with prior year directories and rosters.

Additional explanations of each type of information are shown below:

☆ QUICK REFERENCE INFORMATION

The majority of Quick Reference Information you need can be stored in the Contacts or Calendar app of your smartphone or in your physical calendar (if you use one).

- **Personal calendar:** Keep your calendar up-to-date.
- **Contact Information** is one of the largest categories of information that you'll need constantly. It needs to be kept up-to-date not only for your family, friends, and doctors but also for coaches, teachers, and others

associated with your child's activities and organizations that you or your family are a part of. Include babysitters, caregivers, people who support your household (as applicable), repairmen, cleaners, gardeners, as well as contacts for your financial and insurance accounts. Keep this information updated in your smartphone.

- **Access Information** for websites and apps. Save user IDs and passwords for healthcare, insurance, financial providers, and more.
- **Quick Reference Information Documents**
  - In some instances, I found it was helpful to create a summary document of the information I wanted to be able to access quickly. Examples of these include our monthly household budget, my children's activity rosters, and a list of monthly dates to remember. You can store the document in a variety of ways:
  - Import the document to your Notes app on your smartphone.
  - Create a PDF to upload to the cloud.
  - Take a photo of the document to keep in your smartphone.

Your quick reference information will be invaluable; you will access it more than you might think and will be glad to have it. You'll find fast answers to questions and simplify making plans. These are small things, but small things add up to greatly affect your ability to get things done and make your life less hectic and more pleasant. See Box: *Using Quick Reference Information.*

USING QUICK
REFERENCE INFORMATION

○ **Forming a Car Pool:** You might talk with other parents when you come to pick up your child after an activity and discuss setting up a carpool. If you have the activity roster of names and addresses, you can determine which families would work well to carpool based on their address.

○ **Getting to Know Parents and Their Children:** A copy of the activity roster will allow you to sort out which child goes with which parent. Since you will share time frequently, you'll be glad to connect with parents and their children without having to constantly ask for their names. If you're like me, you'll find that it's easy to forget names when you're speeding from one activity to the next. Some parents will become good friends, especially if your children continue together in a par-ticular activity, year after year.

○ **Knowing Which Child Is Which:** It's nice to have a roster that has children's names and their corresponding team number. This way, you can be certain which child is making a play, scoring a goal, making a point or a pass, etc. On more than one occasion, I found myself at an event watching or rooting for the "wrong" child because the children looked very much alike in their uniforms.

☆ CURRENT-TERM REFERENCE INFORMATION

This is information you need to save for the current period, semester, or year. This information will be relevant to activities, teams, classes, etc. in which you or your child are presently involved. You can store the information that you don't need to see as often in physical files and notebooks, or in computer files or folders. You can refer to this information as needed during the current period, such as your child's current year class curriculum.

☆ LONG-TERM REFERENCE

This is information to save indefinitely for reference. Long-term information can include health records, financial and insurance information, household files, and more. Your child's immunization records and family legal documents are good examples of reference information to keep long-term. Some current-period information will become long-term reference information at the end of the season or school year. For example, the most recent team roster or school directory will become long-term reference information to keep.

You can use any combination of methods to store information, from physical files and notebooks to online files and scans of documents. You'll also be able to retrieve information online. I use a mix of these, depending on the category. For family health information, I store notes from appointments with doctors and other health-care visits in individual files for each family member, and I also access information through online patient portals. For social information, I use small notebooks with tabs. For tax files, I store current year tax receipts in online and physical files and copies of annual tax returns in PDFs (Portable Document Formats) on my computer.

Use the storage methods that work best for you. The main idea is to have the information you need where you can access it when you need it. Try to keep your information and storage up-to-date. Your life will be simplified by having a well-maintained and reliable system for keeping track of your family information.

☆ EMERGENCY REFERENCE GUIDE

Create an Emergency Reference Guide to post in your home. Include the information shown in the guide below.

EMERGENCY REFERENCE GUIDE	
Emergency—Call 911	**Poison Control Number**
Pediatrician Hours Phone Number Address	**Ob/Gyn Doctor** Phone Number Address
Primary Family Doctor Phone Number Address	**Pediatric Dentist** Phone Number Address
After Hours Emergency Care Hours Phone Number Address	**Local Hospital** Emergency Phone Number Address
Urgent Care Hours Phone Number Address	**Pharmacy** Hours Phone Number Address

(continued on next page) ▶

▶ *(continued from previous page)*

EMERGENCY REFERENCE GUIDE	
Local Fire Station Phone Number Address	**Local Police Station** Phone Number Address
Mom's Cell Number	**Mom's Work Number**
Dad's Cell Number	**Dad's Work Number**
Caregiver Phone Number Address	**Day Care** Phone Number Address
Neighbors Phone Number Phone Number Address	**Neighbors** Phone Number Phone Number Address

☆ HEALTH-CARE NOTES FORM

Take notes at health-care appointments. Use this form as a guide. Before you go to the appointment, write down any questions or observations that you'd like to ask or discuss. Summarize the appointment with brief notes. Be sure to note any follow-up action required and calendar the follow-up date as a reminder.

HEALTH-CARE NOTES	
Name	Date

Doctor/Other Health Provider

Questions/Observations to Discuss

Weight:
Height:
Immunizations:

Notes and Follow-Up Instructions

Follow-Up Date: (if needed)	Next Appointment Date

ACKNOWLEDGMENTS

To my husband George, thank you for your constant love and support and for sharing your big heart and life with me. I love your devotion to our family and that you've always been a hands-on and incredible dad. To my children, Emily and Alex, my loves, it's been quite a journey; being your mom has filled my heart and life with so much joy and delight. Keep being your kind and caring selves and I will always be here to love and celebrate you. To my dear sister, Margaret Lynn who I've always looked up to, I'm so lucky to have you as a role model and my cheerleader. I thank each of you for encouraging me to write; your support has meant everything to me.

Thank you to Book Passage, our wonderful community, independent bookstore, for offering writing classes and your program, *Path to Publishing*. Leslie Keenan, your writing class, "Is there a Book in You?" was the spark that made me start and continue to write the book I'd been carrying in my head. To my classmates and authors, Christine Mann, Janis Radar, and Marinda Freeman, your writing was an inspiration for me. I loved the years of sharing Friday morning class with you. Thank you for your encouragement as well as your kind and helpful feedback.

Thank you to author, Tara Mohr for believing in me and telling me, early on, "you are an author." Thank you to my friends at The Hivery for your support. Thank you to Brooke Warner of She Writes Press for seeing the promise in my book and for publishing *The ABCs of Being Mom*.

I appreciate the many experts whose books on parenting and children's physiological and emotional development helped me to decipher and understand my children's growth. I am especially grateful to the authors whose books spoke to me as a mom, prompting me to think deeply about what I wanted for our family. Thank you Wendy Mogel for your book, *The Blessing of a Skinned Knee*, Mary Pipher for your book *The Shelter of Each Other* and Madeline Levine for your book, *The Price of Privilege*.

Last but by no means least, thank you to my dear friends who shared the early years of motherhood with me and made me a better mom. I cherish those times. Kristen, Paula, Janet, Judi, Mary, Margaret, Lesli and Thana, you will always be in my heart.

ABOUT THE AUTHOR

Karen Bongiorno is a mother of two children, a daughter and a son, who have both graduated from college and launched independently. Before motherhood, she had a career in private banking in Los Angeles and on Wall Street in New York. During her child-raising years, she started up and ran a small business and wrote books for moms. She also volunteered in her community, working many hours in local children's and parents' organizations and raising funds for local philanthropies and her children's schools and activities. Her child-raising years were often filled with worry and the overriding question of, "Now what?!" This book is her answer to those concerns. After completing this book, Karen passed away unexpectedly on February 4, 2021. She lived with her husband, George, in Marin County, California, and with their beloved dog, Charlie, until his passing in June 2020.

Author photo © Sophia Mavrides